This book may be kept

FOURTEEN DAYS

A fine will be charged for each day the book is kept overtime.

DEC 1969			
JAN 1 6 1970			
MAR 2 1970			
APR 1 5 1970			
MAY 2 0 1970			
MAY 1 2 1971			
OCT 1 5 1971			
DEC 1 0 1971			
JAN 2 5 1972			
'AY 1 5 1972			
NOV 9 1979			
MAR 3 1 1980			
OCT 1 2 '88			
MAY 1 7 '89			

GAYLORD 142

Books by Hal Butler

The Bob Allison Story
The Harmon Killebrew Story
There's Nothing New In Sports

The
Bob Allison Story

From early childhood, Bob Allison set his sights on a baseball career. Even when he attended a high school that had no baseball team, and he starred in football, basketball and track, and later became a star fullback at the University of Kansas, his aim never wavered. When he accepted a contract from the then Washington Senators, it seemed his ambition was fulfilled. But in reality, his greatest challenge still lay ahead. For now Allison was no longer the outstanding athlete of his small town, but one of hundreds of players vying for the major leagues. Highlighting Bob Allison's most spectacular achievements, while giving fascinating glimpses of his fellow players and of his team's drive to the top of the league, this book does not recount any sudden breakthrough or overnight triumph. Instead it is an account of hard work, unsparing self-criticism, fierce determination in the face of injury and temporary setback, and step-by-step progress toward the eminence that Bob Allison has come to enjoy. Here is the true feel of a big league ballplayers's life in a book that tells the story of one man's victory over his own limitations.

Books by Hal Butler

The Bob Allison Story
The Harmon Killebrew Story
There's Nothing New In Sports

Bob Allison,
outfielder Minnesota Twins.

Bob Allison and Harmon Killebrew
with the Washington Senators (1959)
when Allison was a rookie.

Allison in batting action with the
Washington Senators.

The Allison family delighted by the
news that he's been named the American League's "Rookie of the Year"

Allison going for first base in a vain
attempt to keep from being third
out in a triple play in game with
Baltimore.

Allison with seven bats—one for each run he drove in during the first game of a doubleheader with the Baltimore Orioles.

Allison scores for the Twins in a slide safe at home.

A bases loaded single by Allison in the eighth inning, and five-hit pitching by Pascual defeated the New York Yankees in a night game 4-2.

Bob Allison, Pedro Ramos, Reno Bertoia, heroes of the 6-0 opening day victory over the New York Yankees (1961).

Allison climbs the fence for a catch but all he gets is a better view of homer by Frank Robinson of the

The
Bob Allison Story

by HAL BUTLER

Illustrated with photographs

Julian Messner · New York

Published simultaneously in the United States and
Canada by Julian Messner, a division of Simon &
Schuster, Inc., 1 West 39 Street, New York, N. Y. 10018.
All rights reserved.
Copyright, ©, 1967 by Hal Butler

Printed in the United States of America
Library of Congress Catalog Card No. 67-21611

In Memory of
My Mother

The
Bob Allison Story

1

The hot Missouri sun, a blazing ball in a brittle blue sky, poured down its scorching rays on an already parched earth. No rain had fallen for more than a week, and the earth was dry and sandy.

Eight-year-old Bob Allison jammed the three-pronged fork into the ground alongside the potato row and turned the dirt carefully. Then he dropped to his knees, dug into the loose earth with his fingers and extracted several potatoes. He tossed them into a basket and sat back to wipe perspiration from his forehead with a handkerchief.

"Whew—it's hot!" he remarked.

Bob's father, working another row, grinned.

"Take a rest, son, if you want," he said. "Don't tire yourself out."

"I won't," said Bob quickly. Then a sudden thought occurred to him. "You gonna hit me some flies tonight, Dad?"

Bob's father chuckled. "Never too tired to play ball, eh, Bob?"

He was fond of his young son who, even at the age of eight,

showed a ripening interest in baseball. As a semipro catcher himself, the elder Allison looked forward to developing Bob into a good ballplayer.

"Yes," he said. "I'll hit you some. I'll run your legs off."

Young Allison returned to his work with a new feeling of contentment. He was wild about baseball. Every moment he could spare from school or work on his father's farm, he was either playing baseball with the kids in nearby Raytown, Missouri, or shagging flies hit to him by his father.

That evening, when the necessary farm chores were finished, Bob "ran his legs off" chasing flies. It was a stiff workout. His father hit fungoes to right and left of him, brought Bob in on short ones and chased him back on long towering rainmakers.

When it was over, young Bob came trotting in, his face beaded with sweat.

"You've got to learn to go back on them," his father said. "That's the toughest play for an outfielder—getting away with the crack of the bat, turning his back to the ball and reaching up at the right instant to snag it. We'll work some more on those."

Bob nodded. He knew he needed practice, and he was willing to work at it. In a few years he hoped to be playing semipro ball, like his father, and after that he wanted to go on to minor league ball—and, someday, the majors.

Even at the age of eight, Bob Allison had set his course in life. He was determined to be a big league ballplayer.

William Robert (Bob) Allison was born on July 11, 1934, in Raytown, Missouri, a suburb of Kansas City. He was the first child of Robert Louis Allison and his wife, Frances Louise. Two years after Bob was born the couple had a second son, James Dean, and a year later a daughter, Frankie Lou.

The Allisons were a typical hardworking American family with a small amount of money and a great amount of courage. The elder Allison had battled his way through the dark days of the depression, and, in the process, had migrated from Linwood, Kansas, to Raytown, where job opportunities seemed more plentiful. At the time of Bob's birth he was working in a steel construction job—hard, tough work that put muscles in his arms and meat on his table.

Bob's early boyhood was a combination of school, baseball and work, with the emphasis on work. When he was six or seven years old he often labored on weekends and during summer vacation on nearby farms, picking tomatoes and other vegetables to help the family financially. When he was eight the family moved to a farm of their own, just outside Raytown, and "chores" became a way of life to Bob.

But despite work, he still had time in those early days for baseball. Exposed to the game at a tender age, it wasn't long before baseball became a driving force in his young life. His father was a catcher for the Blue Valley semipro team that played its games in and around Raytown on Sundays, and Bob always attended the games. By the time he was seven years old he was serving the team as a batboy, and at eight he was playing choose-up baseball on the vacant lots of Raytown at every opportunity.

Bob Allison's first experience as a player in organized ball came at the age of eleven when he joined a Peewee League team. Even at this age Bob was a little bigger and more muscular than most of his teammates and gave promise of becoming a big-boned youth who might someday develop along the classic lines of a slugger. But he had more than size. He had natural ability and a strong dedication to the game, and it was these attributes that brought him to the attention of Albert Oetting, a teacher at Raytown High School and manager of a sandlot team.

"The Reitz Meat Company is sponsoring a sandlot baseball team," Oetting told him. "How about joining the team, Bob?"

"I'd sure like to," Bob said enthusiastically.

"I've been watching you," said Oetting. "You play the outfield well, and you're big enough to make a good target at first base. You'll fit in at one of those places."

As it turned out, Bob played both positions for the Reitz Meat Company and did a good job at each. Oetting saw Bob's potential from the start and took an interest in teaching him some of the fine points of baseball. By the time Bob reached high school age, his ability on the ball field was sufficient for him to make any high school baseball team in the country.

This was just fine except for one thing. Raytown High School had no baseball team!

Most big league ballplayers have had the advantage of playing baseball in high school, but Bob Allison never did. When he entered Raytown High in 1948, he felt frustrated by the fact that the school had no baseball team.

"That's the game I really want to play," he told his father, "and three or four years of high school baseball would help me a lot."

Mr. Allison recognized his son's love for baseball, and he was just as determined as Bob to see that he made progress in the game.

"I'd suggest you go out for football and basketball at Raytown High," he said. "All sports are valuable because they teach the importance of teamwork and they help you to develop physically. You can always play sandlot ball in your spare time."

"I guess it's the only thing to do," Bob agreed.

Shortly after entering Raytown High School, Bob reported for basketball. Coach Ted Chittwood, who handled all sports at the school, looked him over carefully. Bob was not, as yet, a fully developed specimen of manhood. At the age of fourteen, he was still in his growth years. Although inclined to lankiness —which gave promise that someday he would be a tall young man—he weighed only 115 pounds.

"We can carry you on the squad as a freshman if you can do

the job for us," Chittwood said, "but I think we'll have to get you a special suit."

"I'd like to go out for football too," Bob said.

Chittwood looked dubious. He was certain that Bob would have to grow and put on weight to take the hard knocks of football battle.

"We'll see," he said evasively.

As things turned out, Bob Allison developed into one of Raytown High School's superior athletes, starring in basketball, football and track. Each year he sprouted taller and gained weight. By the time he was a senior he was six feet two and a half inches tall and weighed 185 pounds.

Bob's continuous and steady growth pleased Chittwood and gave Bob a number of advantages as a high school athlete. In basketball, his height meant that he was tall enough to shoot over the defense or tip the ball into the basket under the boards. His added weight made it easier for him to dribble around a defender and drive in on the basket. As a result, he developed into a high scorer who could shoot accurately from inside or outside the "question mark" area, and in one contest he set a scoring record for the school of 35 points. He was also one of the best defensive players in the Kansas City area, going up high and picking rebounds off the backboards consistently.

By the time he finished his basketball career, Bob had become the highest scorer in the school's history and had won four letters in the sport.

Football was another matter. Chittwood had grave doubts that Bob was big enough to play the game. Yet there was so much potential in him that he was suited up and turned loose on the gridiron. It was a lucky thing for Raytown High that he was. Bob played left halfback on both offense and defense. During his three years on the gridiron he became one of Raytown High's outstanding players. He was tall enough to excel in pass defense and fast enough to come up and meet the running plays at the line of scrimmage. A natural team leader, he called all the offensive plays from the halfback spot. On offense he tossed most of the team's passes, and as he gained weight, he became a superior runner.

During the 1949 season the Raytown Bluejays were undefeated, losing only one postseason game. In 1950 the Bluejays won ten and lost one, then added a postseason bowl game to the win column. In 1951 the team played an independent schedule, again going undefeated and winning the Marble Bowl game.

Bob Allison contributed generously to this fine record. He scored 78 points during his junior year and 96 during his senior year. In the latter year he also completed 35 out of 48 passes.

He won three letters in football at Raytown High, and when the football portion of his career ended Chittwood said, "I think Bob was probably the top football player in the entire Kansas City area. His leadership ability was the greatest of any boy we have had in my twenty years at Raytown High School."

This was the first mention of Bob's leadership qualities, but others were to comment similarly throughout his athletic career.

Although Bob was not as fond of track as he was of basketball and football, still he earned three letters on the cinders. But it was track that caused the only real dispute between Bob and Coach Chittwood. Chittwood kept urging him to participate in track, but Bob backed away because it interfered with his sand-lot baseball career. By this time in his high school career, Bob was playing sandlot ball in the Kansas City and Raytown areas during his spare time, and he disliked giving up any baseball time for the sake of track. Still he felt that he owed a lot to Chittwood, and he made every effort to compete in track. The result was that he would often take off from a track meet to play base-ball, thus participating in two sports in one day.

At any rate, Bob was good enough on the cinder tracks to run in the 100-, 200- and 440-yard dashes and also to participate in the broad jump and discus throw.

But his true love was baseball, and on the sandlots he was

making noticeable progress in the game. He played American Legion ball where he was managed by his father, industrial league ball, and with the Les Milgram Food Stores team in the Ban Johnson League, a strong amateur loop in the Kansas City area.

It was in the Ban Johnson League that Bob profited from some advice on hitting offered by manager Alex George. George was aware of the power and potential that Allison had, but he felt it was being wasted by Bob's overeagerness to hit the pitch.

"You're too anxious," George told him. "You're trying to knock every ball out of the lot. Just swing for hits, and a lot of them will go out of the park anyway. And don't swing at everything the pitcher throws. Wait for a good pitch."

It was good advice and Bob tried it, with the result that his hitting improved.

At the time, Kansas City was one of the hottest sandlot areas in the country. Players who could do well in the Kansas City sandlot leagues were considered big league prospects, and scouts from major league clubs beat a path to the big midwestern city every summer.

Nor did they overlook the big rawboned athlete from Raytown. Scouts were in the stands at many games in which Bob played, and they took a careful look at his hitting, fielding and running. Most of them liked what they saw, but for some time no firm offer was made. The scouts seemed willing to bide their time until this still-growing high school boy reached his maximum height and weight, when he might begin to realize some of the potential they all thought he had.

Meantime, football scouts were busy watching Allison, too. They came from the University of Oklahoma, University of Kansas and Kansas State to see his performance on the Raytown High School gridiron. And they offered football scholarships. When Bob graduated from high school in 1952 he was confronted with a dilemma.

"It's baseball I want to play," he said to his father. "But nobody has offered me a baseball scholarship at any school. What do you think I ought to do?"

"I'd accept a football scholarship," his father advised. "A good education will never hurt you, and you can continue to play sandlot ball. One of these days a baseball scout at one of your games is going to make an offer."

"What school do you think I ought to go to?" Bob asked.

The elder Allison grinned. "As you know, I've always been a Jayhawker myself. I'd make it the University of Kansas."

2

Bob Allison enrolled at the University of Kansas in Lawrence in the fall of 1952. He immediately reported for freshman football and in 1953 moved up to the varsity as a powerful 210-pound fullback. In his sophomore year he established himself as one of the fastest backs in the Big Eight Conference, and he earned scattered All-Conference mention at the end of the season. But the Kansas University Jayhawks didn't make much of a splash as a team—winning four and losing six—and this prevented Bob from reaping higher honors.

During his two years in college, Bob was a young man beset with a puzzling problem. He enjoyed football, and most of his college honors came from this sport, but baseball was his first love. He dreamed of the time when he would walk out on a major league diamond as a member of an honest-to-goodness big league team. He was not brash about this. He simply had a quiet confidence in his own ability, and he strongly believed that a man was capable of accomplishing anything he set out to do if he applied himself relentlessly to the task. He had a determination to excel at anything he tried, whether it was baseball,

football or a quiet game of cards. He had a winning complex
and he wanted to be the best.

While Bob was distinguishing himself on the gridiron during
his sophomore year at the University of Kansas, he received
a letter from the professional San Francisco 49ers. It was a questionnaire asking him, among other things, if he would be interested in playing professional football.

Bob sat down and filled out the questionnaire carefully. Then
he added a note: "Yes, I would be interested in playing pro
football, *if I can't make it in baseball.*"

This statement may have discouraged the 49ers, because it
was the last he heard from them.

Luckily for Bob, big league baseball scouts watching him on
the Kansas City sandlots weren't giving up so easily. During his
last two years in high school and his first two years in college,
they continually buzzed around his door. Altogether, there were
six teams interested in the big brawny right-handed hitter—the
Washington Senators, New York Yankees, St. Louis Cardinals,
Cleveland Indians, Philadelphia Phillies and the old Boston
Braves. Of the six, the Senators and the Yankees were the most
persistent.

One day Tom Greenwade, the famous Yankee scout who six
years earlier had discovered Mickey Mantle, called on Bob. He
was armed with some enticing information about how smart it
would be for Bob to sign with the perennial champion New York
Yankees.

"Of course," he said, "we can't offer more than four thousand
dollars as a bonus for signing. I think you understand the reason
for this."

Bob understood. The year was 1954, and a big league ruling
was making large bonuses a rarity. Any team that offered a
player a bonus of more than $4000 was required to keep him
in the majors for two years before sending him out for minor
league experience. In most cases, this arrangement was unfair to
both the club and the player. The club had to keep a raw rookie

who couldn't help them on the bench for two years. The player was handicapped by idling away his time instead of gaining experience in a minor league. Because of this ruling, none of the clubs offered him more than the maximum of $4000.

"However," Greenwade went on, "there are a lot of good reasons why you should join the Yankees. The Yankee ball club is a fine organization. They're a strong club, always in the pennant fight. You'll be able to increase your pay considerably with all the World Series checks you'll be collecting as a member of a pennant winner."

"How do you know the Yanks will continue to win the pennant?" Bob asked.

"It's pretty much a cinch," said Greenwade with unbridled confidence. "Look at the last five years—1949 through 1953. Won the pennant every time."

"Well," said Allison uncertainly, "I'll have to think it over, Mr Greenwade. I've had some other offers and I'm just going to have to take the time to decide."

It was a tough choice for Bob Allison to make. Several clubs had offered him the same $4000 to sign, and the Yankees held out the lure of more money from World Series checks. But Bob was in a hurry. He wanted to make it with a big league club and make it as quickly as possible. And the Yankees, to Bob, seemed like the toughest club of all to make in a hurry. They were so loaded with talent that it might take years for him to make a dent in the Yankee lineup, whereas some of the other clubs—like Washington, for example—seemed to offer better prospects for quick advancement.

The Washington Senators, as a matter of fact, appealed strongly to young Bob. Their team record was nowhere near as impressive as the Yankees'. They had been in the second division for the past seven years—three times they had finished fifth, three times seventh and one time last. They could use new talent and use it quickly.

Apparently Bob Allison appealed to the Washington Senators

too, because their scout, Ray Baker, had been one of the most persistent. He was unable to tempt Bob with World Series checks, but he offered the same $4000 that everyone was offering and he had another talking point that Bob considered important.

"You'll get a chance to play sooner with the Senators than with any other team," he said. "A year or so in the minors, maybe, and you'll be up with us. We need guys who can hit the ball, and you look like you'd do our club a lot of good."

It was late 1954 and Bob Allison was now just twenty years old. He had a lot of confidence in his father's opinion on baseball matters, and one day he sat down with his Dad and discussed all the pros and cons of the offers that had been made,

"I have a year and a half to go to get a degree in physical ed at University of Kansas," Bob said. "Maybe I should finish college before I sign with a ball club. Still, I've always wanted to be a big league ballplayer, and I hate to pass up an opportunity."

The elder Allison knew that Bob loved baseball, and that with his determination there was every likelihood that he would succeed in the majors. He saw no reason to hold his son up in a career he wanted so desperately to follow.

"I think you ought to sign a baseball contract," he advised. "Then you can go back and finish your education in the off-season."

Bob took his father's advice. In January, 1955, Ray Baker of the Senators brought a big league contract to the Allison home. With the stroke of a pen, the big broad-shouldered sandlot outfielder became the property of the Washington Senators, the team Bob felt would give him the quickest opportunity to play in the major leagues.

Although Bob wasn't aware of it at the time, the Senators had signed another young man six months before, Harmon Killebrew. In time, these two young athletes, Killebrew and Allison, were to become the two greatest sluggers on the Washington ball club.

But that was not to happen for four long years, and in the

meantime both players were to experience a discouraging series of ups and downs.

Bob Allison had more than one reason for happiness in January, 1955. Not only did he sign his first major league contract, but he also took another important step that was to make a significant change in his life. He became engaged to an attractive young lady named Betty Shearer, a former Raytown High School beauty queen and Bob's sweetheart for several years.

Shortly thereafter Bob Allison reported to the Washington Senators' minor league training camp at Winter Garden, Florida. When he walked onto the field for the first time, Allison's heart pounded a little harder than was normal. He knew that he was making his first critical move toward the big leagues, and he knew that he would now have to show what he had to offer to the Washington Senators.

The Winter Garden layout was a tidy one where the Senators carefully examined all of their best minor league prospects, as well as their just-signed rookies. Those considered not ready for a tryout at the Senators' camp at Orlando were then assigned to a minor league club in a classification where the Washington brass thought they would best develop.

Bob was a diamond in the rough. His potential was immediately recognized in camp, but he was an incomplete ballplayer who had much to learn. He listened to advice and applied himself vigorously, and when the time came for a decision by the Washington management it was decreed that the diamond needed polishing in Class B ball. Allison reported in the spring to the Hagerstown Packets in the Piedmont League.

Johnny Welaj, manager of the Packets, greeted the husky Allison with a firm handshake.

"We can use a big guy like you," he said, scanning the broad shoulders and muscular arms.

"I hope I can help," said Bob.

Welaj watched Allison closely, taking note of his range in

the field and the power in his throwing arm. Finally he made a decision.

"I'm going to put you in center field," he said. "You have a great arm and you throw a ball like a bullet. You're fast, too, and should be able to cover the ground out there. But I'm going to work with you, Bob. There's still a lot you need to learn about fielding."

Welaj, once an outfielder with the Senators himself, worked diligently with the twenty-year-old outfielder. The two had many practice sessions in which Allison learned that there was a great deal more to playing the outfield than he had ever imagined on the Kansas City sandlots!

"First of all," said Welaj, "you have to learn to get a jump on the ball. If you don't, some that might be caught are going to get away from you. You'll have to learn the hitters, too, know whether they pull the ball, hit straightaway or hit to the opposite field. Part of getting the jump on a fly ball is in being positioned in the right place to begin with. Then, when the ball's hit, you head immediately for the spot where you know that fly ball will come down. After a lot of practice, this will become instinctive."

Allison was proud of his powerful arm, and he uncorked throws at times that brought a murmur of respect from the stands. But he found to his surprise that Welaj had some constructive criticism to give him in this area too.

"You've got a fine arm," Welaj told him. "But this doesn't mean you're obligated to thrill the crowd with a heave from deep center all the way into the plate. Let's suppose there's a runner tagging up at third with a fly ball heading your way. If it's a routine fly ball you can get set for, don't stand flatfooted and catch it. Catch the ball moving in. In other words, back off a step or two, and as the ball comes down, move in on it. That puts you in a position to throw and saves a precious second that can mean the difference between throwing the runner out at the plate or missing him.

"Another thing. When you move in on the ball with a throw to make, try to catch the ball over your right shoulder. This means your arm is already near throwing position, and you can get the throw away quicker. Any extra motion you can eliminate is important, because in the big leagues you'll find that an alert base runner will take advantage of the least little mistake you make."

It all made wonderful sense to Allison. He shook his head in dismay.

"I never learned these things on the sandlots," he said. "Or if I did, they weren't drilled into me, and I've forgotten them. Anyway, I'll sure work at these things you've been telling me."

"I know you will," said Welaj, and there was a note of respect in his voice. Welaj had already spotted one important trait in Allison's makeup that would be a major factor in his eventual climb to the big leagues.

"He has a terrific desire to excel at this game," he told a sportswriter one day. "The kid works his tail off. He listens, he learns, and he applies what he learns. There's nothing in his life more important to him than being a great ballplayer—and that desire is going to pay off for him."

The payoff, however, wasn't immediate. Although Allison learned the intricacies of outfield play and learned them well, he found it more difficult to learn the mysteries of hitting. Despite his muscular build—which gave promise that he might become an outstanding long-ball hitter—he was unimpressive in his first minor league year. In 446 times at bat, he had 114 hits for a so-so average of .256. There were only five homers, two triples and fifteen doubles in those 114 hits, and he drove in a meager 49 runs.

It was hardly enough to cause heart palpitation in the front office of the Washington Senators. But at home in Raytown, Missouri, when Bob returned that fall, he was greeted as something of a hero.

Allison didn't feel the part. "I've got to do a lot better if I'm going to make the grade with the Senators," he told his father.

"Don't worry, you will," the elder Allison replied. "It takes time to develop. Just stick at it, Bob."

While Bob was relaxing in Raytown, two changes occurred in the management of the Washington Senators. On October 27, 1955, Clark Griffith, eighty-five-year-old president of the club, passed away. Calvin Griffith, his nephew, immediately took over the reins.

This change was followed by another. Charlie Dressen, manager of the Senators, was moved into an office job with the organization, and the field leadership was assumed by Cookie Lavagetto.

Allison reflected on what these changes might mean to his career, but decided that they would have relatively little influence. After all, he was not yet a member of the Washington club, and no matter who was manager of the team or who sat in the president's chair, he would still have to show by his performance on the field that he was qualified for a regular job.

However, there was a hidden benefit for Allison in the changes. Calvin Griffith was to become one of Bob Allison's staunchest supporters and was to help him immensely in his climb up baseball's difficult ladder.

February 10, 1956, was a red-letter day in the life of Bob Allison. On that date he married Elizabeth Jane (Betty) Shearer, his high school sweetheart. The couple were wed at the Reorganized Latter-Day Saints Church in Independence, Missouri, and shortly thereafter Bob took his bride to Florida where he again reported to the Winter Garden training camp.

Allison had no idea where he would end up in 1956. He was not sure whether his performance with the Hagerstown Packets had been strong enough to get him a promotion to Class A ball. As a matter of fact, the Washington management wasn't sure either. When Allison's name came up for review there were mixed feelings about him.

"His hitting is a question mark," said Lavagetto.

"Yes, it is," agreed Calvin Griffith, "but he's big and powerful and he should hit. Rollie Hemsley, down in Charlotte, used to be a pretty good hitter. Why don't we send him down there and see if Rollie can help him?"

"Class A?" Lavagetto said dubiously.

"Let's try it," said Griffith.

So when spring training ended at Winter Garden, Bob Allison was told to report to the Charlotte Hornets in the Class A South Atlantic (Sally) League. And Betty went with him to assure him the kind of moral support he needed.

Charlotte, North Carolina, was a hot southern town with a population of about 100,000 contented souls. Manager Rollie Hemsley, a former American League catcher, had been instructed to work with Bob Allison on his hitting, and he appraised the young athlete with a calculating eye. He observed, as others had, that Allison had the classic build of a slugger— broad shoulders, powerful arms, thick wrists—but he also had a major weakness. He wanted to use those shoulders, arms and wrists to knock every pitch out of the park.

"Still, we ought to be able to make something out of this kid," Hemsley told one of his coaches.

Hemsley tried. He worked hard with Allison and he gave him sound advice.

"Don't overswing," he said. "Don't try to kill the ball. Just meet it. You've got the power to drive the ball out of the park, if you just hit it where it's pitched. Think with the pitcher. Know what he throws in the clutch, what his favorite pitch is. Keep your head down, eye on the ball. Get snap into your wrists."

It was all fine advice, but the difference between knowing what to do and doing it is sometimes a wide one. Bob worked hard at it, but improvement with the bat was frighteningly slow.

One day in June a new member joined the Charlotte club. He was a five-foot-eleven solidly built chunk of a man named Harmon Killebrew. After spending two years on the Washington bench, he had been sent down to Charlotte for more seasoning.

"You two guys get acquainted," Hemsley said to Allison and Killebrew. "You'll be roomies on the road."

Allison took an immediate liking to the modest and unassuming Killebrew. "How is it up there in the big leagues?" he asked.

Killebrew smiled wryly. "Oh, it's great, all right. The ball parks are beautiful and you travel first class and you see the greatest players of the day in action. But when you're sitting on the bench all the time—well, it takes some of the thrill out of it."

When Killebrew began hitting with some consistency at Charlotte, Allison, always anxious to learn, pried him with questions about his hitting.

"I'm not much of an authority," Harmon said. "After all, this is the first time I've played regularly in three years. Maybe that's the answer, playing every day."

Toward the end of the season Killebrew was recalled by the Senators, but not Allison. Bob was happy for Killebrew, but not exactly satisfied wtih his own situation.

"You'll make it," he said to Harmon.

"You will too,' said Killebrew. "You've got what it takes."

But Bob Allison, already an excellent fielder and a good base runner, had an unimpressive season in the hitting department. His batting average slipped to .233; he had only 12 home runs and drove in only 55. He went home in the fall feeling a little discouraged by his showing, but his determination was not lessened.

"I'm going to be a big league player," he said to Betty one day. "I'm firmly convinced that a man can do anything if he

wants to do it badly enough. And I want to become a big
league ballplayer as much as anything in the world."

"Don't worry about it, Bob," Betty assured him. "You're going
to make it. I haven't any doubt about it."

It was music to Bob's ears, and he appreciated Betty's wifely
confidence in him. But he hoped that someday he would hear
a baseball manager say the same thing.

3

During the winter months some hardheaded conferences were held in the offices of the Washington Senators. More than a small part of the discussions dealt with Bob Allison. His two-year record in the minors was not exceptional. Although he had all the physical attributes needed by a major league out-fielder—size, power, a good throwing arm, speed—his hitting put him in the doubtful category. Batting .256 at Hagerstown and .233 at Charlotte was hardly a promising start, and the idea was getting around that Allison might never learn to hit minor league pitching, much less the major league variety.

But, strangely, the Washington brass was still high on the young man. This was especially true of Calvin Griffith, one of the rare club owners who was a good judge of baseball ivory.

"I may be wrong," he said once, "but I think this boy is going to hit. Let's try him at Chattanooga."

So it was that Bob Allison found himself, in the spring of 1957, with the Chattanooga Lookouts in the Class AA Southern League. With him were his wife and a brand new son, born on March 3, 1957, and named Robert Mark.

The Chattanooga Lookouts played in a ball park that could turn a right-handed hitter completely cold. In left field, 385 feet away, was a towering scoreboard that had to be cleared to register a home run. You could drive the ball out of the park in center and right field, but left field presented such a formidable barrier that *nobody had ever cleared the scoreboard in the history of the park!*

Cal Ermer, manager of the Lookouts, saw Allison and Harmon Killebrew, who had also been sent to Chattanooga, looking calculatingly at the scoreboard one day.

"Don't worry about it," Ermer said. "Don't let it become a mental hazard. If you pull a line shot into left field you'll get a lot of doubles off that scoreboard, and there are other places in the park where the ball can go into the seats."

Allison glanced at Killebrew. "You might do it, Harm," he said. "You hit those long high flies. But I'm a line-drive type of hitter, and if I ever belt one over that scoreboard it will be a miracle."

The word had come down from the Senators that Allison needed work on his hitting, and early in the 1957 season Ermer concentrated much of his effort on Allison. He would ask Bob to come out to early morning practice, and he would actually stand on the mound and throw to him. Allison would swing until he was dripping with sweat and his arms were growing weak.

"I'm going to make a hitter out of you if it kills us both," Ermer grinned.

"I appreciate all you're doing for me," Bob said. "There's no doubt I need a lot of work."

Under Ermer's urging, Allison's hitting slowly improved, but not to a degree that satisfied the manager. In fact, Ermer couldn't quite see why Allison was failing to live up to his promise as a power hitter. In the field, Bob was near-perfect. He could field, he was fast, he judged a fly ball well, he had a throwing arm among the best in the league, and he could frighten most infielders out of their wits with his reckless base running.

Only his hitting was holding him back.

One day in midseason the strength in Bob Allison's arms and torso was illustrated in different fashion when a flare-up took place between the Lookouts and the New Orleans Pelicans. Tempers were soaring under the hot southern sun, and suddenly Allison saw Peanuts Lowry charge from the Pelicans' dugout with a bat in his hand and a murderous gleam in his eyes. And he was headed straight toward the Lookouts' pitcher!

Bob Allison, normally good-natured, rarely became aroused, but he quickly sensed the danger in the situation. With a burst of speed he raced in from his outfield post. He arrived before Lowry made it as far as the pitcher's mound. With one quick motion he wrapped his thick arms around Lowry and lifted him off the ground. While Lowry kicked and protested, Allison calmly carried him back to the Pelicans' dugout and planted him there.

"Keep him," Allison said.

His action had prevented a serious fight, but it also raised a question in Cal Ermer's mind. "With strength like that, why can't he knock the ball out of the park?" he asked himself.

But knocking the ball out of the park was not one of Bob Allison's talents—at least not in 1957. He ended the season in Chattanooga with only two home runs. His batting average was .246, a slight improvement over the previous year against Class A pitching in Charlotte. And although this wasn't much of a peg to hang his hopes on, Bob nevertheless felt that his hitting had improved sufficiently under Cal Ermer's tutelage that he might, just might, be called up to the Senators in 1958.

Bob Allison was delighted and thrilled when he received word to report in the spring of 1958, not to the minor league camp in Winter Garden, but to the Washington Senators' training camp in Orlando, Florida. Again his wife and young son traveled south with him, and when Allison arrived at the Senators' Tinker Field he had both high hopes and butterflies in his stomach. He was acutely aware that this would be a critical spring for him, because now he would perform on the same field with established major leaguers, and Manager Cookie Lavagetto would inevitably make comparisons.

And the competition, he knew, would be terrific. In the big sprawling training camp were such outstanding players as Jim Lemon, Roy Sievers, Reno Bertoia, Ed Fitzgerald, Ron Samford, Camilo Pascual, Pedro Ramos, Norm Zauchin—all with the ability to stick with the club. Still, there was a chance for him. Roy Sievers and Jim Lemon were obviously going to earn themselves spots in the outfield. But one outfield position was open, and Allison had his eye on it.

Bob Allison worked hard at Tinker Field and, much to his delight, he had a good spring, hitting seven home runs in Grapefruit League games and, in general, deporting himself in a big league manner. Toward the end of the exhibition season, he expressed his joy to Betty.

"I really think I might go north with the club now," he said. "My hitting has improved and that's the thing that's going to count."

"It'll be nice living in Washington," Betty said dreamily.

Then the ax fell mercilessly. Just before the spring training games ended, Bob received a severe jolt to his hopes. The Washington Senators obtained speedy little Albie Pearson in a trade and tagged him for center field.

"I'm sorry," said Lavagetto, "but our outfield is set now, and we're going to have to send you back to Chattanooga. Figure it this way, Bob—it won't hurt you. You'll come back here in 1959 with a much better chance to stick with the club."

Bob was shaken by the turn of events. Gloomily he said goodbye to his friend, Harmon Killebrew, who was going north with the team.

"It's tough," said Harmon sympathetically, "but I know you're going to make it. Next year for sure."

Allison was feeling low. "I don't know, Harm," he said. "I have a wife, a son and a five-hundred-dollar-a-month contract —and I'm not so sure but what I'm a failure at this business."

It was at this point that Bob's morale had reached its lowest ebb. There was no way for it to go but up, and up it went. After the initial shock dissipated itself, Bob's old determination came back again.

"I'm going to show them!" he said to Betty. "I'm going to have a good season with the Lookouts. And when I go back to the Senators' camp next spring, I'll set the place on fire!"

What happened in Chattanooga is now a bright spot in the personal record book of Bob Allison. Red Marion had taken over as manager of the Lookouts, and he continued to work Allison hard in morning practice sessions. This extra work, plus a renewed determination on Allison's part, resulted in a fine 1958 season. Catching fire from the beginning, Allison ended with the highest batting average of his career—a resounding .307. Although the menace of the left-field scoreboard held his home run total to nine, he hit 28 doubles and nine triples and drove in 93 runs!

Allison's fireworks at Chattanooga weren't lost on the Washington management. Calvin Griffith was almost ecstatic, although other members of the brass, including Cookie Lavagetto, were inclined to withhold judgment. Nevertheless, in mid-September Bob Allison received the welcome news that the Senators were calling him up to finish out the season. They wanted a good look at this big Missouri boy whose bat, at long last, was beginning to play a happy tune.

Harmon Killebrew, who had been sent back to Chattanooga in midseason, was also called up for the Senators' closing games. The two players congratulated each other.

"You've been with the Senators," Allison told Killebrew. "But for me it's the first time up. That's going to be quite a thrill."

"I hope we both do well up there, Bob," Harmon said.

Needless to say, both Allison and Killebrew broke all records packing their suitcases and getting out of town. They headed directly for Cleveland where the Washington Senators were meeting the Indians.

The date was September 16, 1958. A twenty-one-year-old rookie named Gary Bell was slated to pitch for the Indians. Allison had faced Bell before in the Southern League and knew he was a tough pitcher with a good fast ball, a slow curve and plenty of control.

"It's a good spot to start you in, Bob," said Lavagetto with vague logic.

Bob's first view of spacious Municipal Stadium in Cleveland gave him exactly the thrill he had anticipated. It was the biggest ball park he had ever seen. The infield was manicured to perfection, and the outfield grass was as smooth as a putting green. He stood on the dugout steps and stared at the field for a long time—and he kept thinking, *so this is the big leagues!*

To his surprise, Bob found himself installed in center field and batting in the leadoff position. That meant he would be the first batter to walk up and test Gary Bell's slants when the umpire said, "Play ball!"

"What's Cookie trying to do, scare me to death?" he asked Killebrew.

"Just relax," said Harmon. "You'll be all right."

From the dugout to the plate was the longest walk Bob Allison had ever taken. Bell, anxious to make good in the majors, tried about everything—a curve on the outside, a fast ball in tight, a couple of wide ones. Bob finally swung and lifted a pop fly back of second. It was an even longer walk back to the dugout.

As it developed, nobody was hitting Gary Bell that day. Herb Plews, the Washington second baseman, got a single in the first inning, but nobody got another hit until the top of the ninth. By that time the score was Cleveland 5, Washington 1, the Senators having scored one run without the aid of a hit.

Bell was working on a one-hitter when Allison faced him in the ninth. Bob had batted three times and had failed to hit. This would be his last chance.

Confident now, Bell threw a fast ball by Allison for the first strike. The next pitch was outside, and Bob let it go for ball one. The next caught the corner for strike two, and Bob stepped out of the box, picked up a little dirt, settled down his jumpy nerves a bit, and got back in.

With two strikes, he had to protect the plate. He waved his bat in a threatening arc. Bell went up with his arm, hesitated, then threw the ball. It came in on the outside corner, a fast ball, and Bob swung. The shock as bat hit ball felt good in his hands and his arms, and the ball traveled on a line into right field.

It was the second hit of the ball game for the Senators, and the first major league hit of Bob Allison's career!

Although the Senators lost the game, 5–1, Bob felt good about his own contribution. He had fielded flawlessly and had poled one of the two hits the Senators collected—and this, Bob thought, was a creditable performance for his first major league game.

That first hit started a streak of four games in which Bob hit safely. The next day, at Fenway Park in Boston, he had one of the five hits the Senators made off Tom Brewer. The following afternoon Washington got only four hits off Frank Sullivan, but one of them was a single by Allison. In the next game he hit another single to run his streak to four games, before being blanked the following afternoon by the Baltimore Orioles.

Unfortunately, none of Bob's hits helped the Senators much. They were in a sad batting slump, starting with Allison's first game. They not only lost all four games, but were held scoreless for thirty-seven consecutive innings!

Allison played in only eleven games for the Washington Senators in 1958, posting seven hits out of thirty-five times at bat for a batting average of .200. These figures meant little, because of the limited number of games involved, but those seven hits gave Bob added encouragement. After all, they had been made off American League pitching, and they would be etched in his memory when he reported to Tinker Field in Orlando for 1959 spring training.

Bob Allison was uncomfortably aware that 1959 would be the most crucial year of his career—the year when he would have to stick with the Senators or slide back into the minors for what could very well be the last time.

"I can't let that happen," he told Betty. "I've got to go down to Orlando next spring and clinch a place on the team. And before I do that, I've got to get all the baseball under my belt that I can get. You know what that means?"

Betty nodded. "You want to play winter ball," she said.

"Right," said Bob. "How would you like to spend the winter in, say, Cuba?"

4

If anybody needed a talented young ballplayer who would "find himself" in 1959, the Washington Senators did. The club had finished deep in the American League cellar in both 1957 and 1958 and had not been out of the second division in twelve years.

All through the winter of 1958–1959 there were substantial rumors floating about the baseball world that the Senators wanted to move out of Washington to greener pastures. The downtrodden club was not drawing enough customers to make the franchise worthwhile, and the owners felt that switching to a new city not only would be a financially sound move but might produce the shot in the arm the ballclub needed to start winning.

For many years big league baseball had maintained the status quo, with the shifting of franchises to different cities a rarity. But this conservatism was dying. Club owners had become restless, and one team after another had sought out new locations. The St. Louis Browns had shifted to Baltimore, the Boston Braves had gone to Milwaukee, and the Philadelphia Athletics had jumped to Kansas City. Even the New York Giants had leaped to San Francisco, and Brooklyn's beloved Dodgers had fled to Los Angeles.

But moving the Senators out of Washington was a slightly different matter. Washington was, after all, the nation's capital, and there was a great amount of sentiment against leaving Washington without a representative in the American League. Calvin Griffith was casting eyes in the direction of Minneapolis–St. Paul, and the Twin Cities were more than willing to accept the Senators. But leaving Washington without a franchise seemed impossible.

The United States Congress was cool to the shift of the Senators from Washington. Legislation was threatened to stop such a move. Even President Dwight D. Eisenhower made it known that he wanted the club to stay in D.C. Reporters kept trying to get Calvin Griffith to make a definite statement on the matter —was he or wasn't he going to move the club out? Griffith was cagey.

"We'll just have to wait and see how things work out," he said.

None of this backstage maneuvering meant much to Bob Allison's budding baseball career. He was going to have to successfully demonstrate his talents on the ball field whether the team played in Washington, Twin Cities, or Timbuktu.

"It doesn't matter *where* I play," he once said, "it matters *how* I play."

To improve his chances, Allison moved his wife and child to Havana, Cuba, that winter and quartered them in a hotel near the airport. This was in the pre-Castro era when baseball was a thriving sport in Cuba, and many talented Cuban players were being gobbled up by American clubs.

Allison signed with the Almendares team in the Cuban League. He found himself among a group of ballplayers whose names he knew well—players who either were eager to increase their chances of making a big league club by playing winter ball, or who were already in the big time and wanted to cement their chances of staying there. Among them were Art Fowler, Willie Miranda, Rocky Nelson, Sandy Amoros, Carlos Paula and Angel Scull. Playing with other teams in the same league were such outstanding performers as Pedro Ramos, Camilo Pascual and Zoilo Versalles.

Bob Allison found the Cuban League to be much tougher than he had imagined. The team played only four times a week, and because of the many off-days it was difficult for a hitter to maintain his timing. The pitchers, with plenty of rest between games, had the advantage. The Cuban League was considered a "pitchers' league," and this was pretty much proved by the fact that there was only one .300 hitter in the entire loop.

Allison started in the Almendares outfield, but when he failed to hit he was benched. He sat forlornly in the dugout, getting none of the experience he was anxious to get and wondering why he couldn't make the grade even in winter ball. While he sat, Sandy Amoros, Carlos Paula and Angel Scull patrolled the outfield. A little later, when Rocky Nelson was injured, Allison took over at first base, but his hitting continued to be a problem that seemed insoluble.

Then came an event in Cuban history that threatened to disrupt all of Allison's carefully laid plans for his 1959 drive to success.

It was New Year's Eve. Bob and Betty had attended a party in a Havana hotel. They were returning with Art Fowler and his wife to their own hotel near the Havana airport in the wee hours of the morning, and as they approached their destination they heard the sounds of roaring airplanes.

"There seems to be an awful lot of activity at the airport," Bob remarked. "What do you suppose is going on?"

Art Fowler shrugged. "Maybe the Cubans celebrate New Year's Eve by taking plane rides. Havana's a pretty gay town!"

The matter didn't seem very important to them at the moment, and they dismissed it from their minds. They said their goodbyes and went to their rooms, where they slept unaware of the monstrous event that was occurring just outside their windows.

It was 10:30 A.M. the next morning when Bob Allison awoke with a start. Obviously, something was going on in the streets below. Bob heard much blowing of horns, shouting, singing— and, more ominously, an occasional sharp report of a gun.

"Something's happening, and I don't like the sound of it," he announced as he leaped out of bed.

Bob and Betty raced to the balcony of their room and looked out. The streets below were a mass of human confusion. Crowds milled around, shouting, waving flags, singing what seemed to be patriotic songs. Automobiles, packed with wild-eyed youths, roared down the streets, blowing horns. But always, in the distance, were the disturbing sounds of gunfire.

"I'm going to find out what's going on," said Allison.

"Be careful, Bob," Betty warned.

"I will."

He dressed quickly and went down to the hotel lobby. A group of men, some Americans, sat in the lobby watching television. The screen was showing a scene somewhat like the one Bob had witnessed from his window.

"What's happening, anyway?" Bob asked of no one in particular.

"We're having a little revolution," said a man with dry humor.

"Revolution?"

"Batista is out," said the man. "Fidel Castro has taken over the government."

It was startling news, and not good news either. Allison thought immediately about the safety of his wife and child. He raced back upstairs and told his wife what was happening.

"I think I know what all the noise at the airport was last night," he said. "Batista and his henchmen were getting out."

He was right. In the small hours of New Year's Day, Dictator Fulgencio Batista had resigned as president of rebellion-torn

Cuba, and he and his supporters had fled to exile in the Dominican Republic. Fidel Castro's rebel forces had seized power, and what was going on in the streets of Havana was something between a celebration and a revolutionary uprising. Years of pent-up emotion had exploded, and people were rioting, breaking windows, smashing up shops and restaurants, and defying police who were trying to maintain order.

Eventually the explosiveness of the situation moderated, but the day of the Castro take-over was followed by a general strike. Stores and restaurants closed. Business stopped. The once gay city of Havana became a grim, silent fortress. Food was scarce. Supplies into the city were curtailed. Havana was suddenly dead.

And, of course, there was no baseball.

For five long days the city was strike-bound. The Allisons and Fowlers had little food, subsisting on cereals and cornmeal. They dared not go out on the streets to seek food, because looting and gunfire were everywhere.

"What a mess!" groaned Fowler. "I thought I was coming down here to improve my chances in baseball. Now we'll be lucky to get back to the States."

It was a hungry ordeal, but eventually the violence in the streets stopped as order was finally restored. Stores opened again and long lines formed to obtain food. The Allisons and Fowlers stood in line for hours to obtain enough food to last a few days. As soon as it was possible, the wives and children were sent back to the States.

After about ten days the Cuban League got back into action again. Allison dressed quietly in the clubhouse, wondering about the temper of the crowd. Would they be the same enthusiastic fans with baseball on their minds, or would the fervor of revolution still be boiling in their blood? Would they be orderly or would they be belligerent?

Allison walked out of the clubhouse and into the dugout— and stopped short. His jaw sagged. At each end of the dugout were bearded Castro soldiers, armed with automatic rifles!

"What's the idea?" he asked Fowler.

"Search me. I don't know if those guns are directed at the crowd or us."

One soldier looked around and regarded the two players curiously. He handled the deadly rifle with ease; its angry snout pointed for a moment in the direction of Allison and Fowler, then swayed back to sweep the field.

"He points that gun around kind of carelessly," said Allison. "It gives me the creeps."

Under the guardianship of the Castroite soldiers, the Almendares team played out the rest of its schedule. On several occasions Fidel Castro himself showed up at the park to receive the wild plaudits of the crowd.

"He's more of a hero than all of us combined," said one player, half-sadly.

"Yeah? How many home runs has he hit?" asked another.

It was a tense situation in which to play baseball, but Almendares played with enough consistency to win the Cuban League title. Then, when the season ended, a team was formed by league members to play in the Caribbean World Series with Puerto Rico, Panama and Caracas, Venezuela. Allison and Fowler, anxious to get as much baseball in as possible, joined. So did the established American League pitching star Camilo Pascual.

In a round-robin playoff, Cuba won all of its games and earned the right to meet Caracas in Venezuela for the title. One game was to be played to determine the Caribbean Championship. That's when Allison experienced his second brush with Latin-American enthusiasm.

When the team arrived at the Caracas ball park, Allison remembered that he was carrying some American money with him.

"I wonder where I could hide this," he said to Fowler. "I don't want to leave it in the locker room."

"I've got some too," said Fowler. "Tell you what. I'll pin it inside the back pocket of my uniform."

"Okay," grinned Allison, handing him the money. "Just don't slide into any bases."

The stadium was packed with a noisy, demonstrative crowd of Caracas fans when the game got under way. Camilo Pascual was on the mound for the Cuban team, and his assortment of fast balls and curves kept the Caracas batters off stride. After seven and a half innings, Cuba was leading 4–0.

Bob Allison was playing in center field, and he had been aware of an angry frustration on the part of the spectators as Pascual continued to mow down the Caracas batters. All of a sudden the anger boiled over. Allison heard an angry roar from behind him and looked back to see a rioting mob climbing over the screen in center and dropping onto the field!

That was enough! Bob and the other outfielders tossed quick glances at each other and then, as if inspired by a single thought, they raced for the dugout. The Cuban infielders also took to their heels, and in a mad dash the Cuban players managed to make the sanctuary of the clubhouse. Doors were slammed shut and locked against the howling mob.

"Holy smokes!" breathed one player. "They meant business out there!"

"They're out of their minds!" said another angrily.

"Do you think they'll break down those doors?"

"I don't think they can."

"I'll bet they'd like to!"

The players huddled in the clubhouse, listening to the angry shouting outside. It was a long time before the mob quieted, but they finally did.

"What now?" a player asked. "Do we get out of this crazy place?"

A uniformed Caracas policeman opened the doors and stepped inside. "We have the crowd under control," he announced simply. "You may finish your game."

Allison felt fright seize him. The umpires were motioning

the players to take the field, and Bob looked at them as if he thought they were completely mad.

"You mean we have to go back out there and finish the last inning and a half?" he asked incredulously.

The answer was yes.

Apprehensively the Cuban team took the field. They were greeted by a cascade of noise and booing, but at least the spectators stayed in their seats.

The game was played to a finish and the Cubans won, and as the last Caracas batter was retired, the frenzied crowd roared to its feet again. Allison and the rest of the team didn't waste any time—they took off in another headlong dash for the clubhouse.

When the players had all showered and were ready to leave, there was a police escort ready for them. As police kept the still-angry crowd back, the players ran for the limousine that would take them to the airport. As Allison climbed into the car a feeling of relief swept over him. But only for a moment. The next thing he knew there were rocks and bricks crashing against the car's sides and windows!

"Let's get out of here!" someone shouted, and the driver gunned the car. It swerved away, leaving the shouting mob behind.

The limousine arrived at the Caracas Airport and the players immediately boarded the plane. A few minutes later it took off, and as the ground fell away beneath him, Allison felt safe for the first time.

"I was never so glad to get off the ground," he said to Fowler.

"Me, too. Remind me never to play in Caracas again, will you?"

They were airborne for some time before a sudden thought occurred to Allison.

"Fowler!"

"What?"

"You didn't leave all our money pinned in your uniform, did you?"

"And leave it in that clubhouse? Not on your life!" Fowler patted his pocket. "I've got it all right here."

Bob Allison was happy that he hadn't lost his money. But he was more happy just to be alive.

5 ⚾

By the time spring training for the 1959 season opened in Orlando, rumors that the Senators were about to desert Washington had dissipated. The American League had notified Calvin Griffith that it would not vote him permission to move his club —and that assured Washington fans of another look at the Senators in 1959.

Bob Allison reported at Tinker Field convinced that this was the year he would stick with the Senators. It wasn't that he minimized the effort it would take. He was well aware that the Senators had a pretty solid outfield with Albie Pearson, Jim Lemon and Roy Sievers, and he knew it would take some doing to run any of these players out of a job. But he was determined to hustle as no rookie before had ever hustled, and he barged into the Senators' camp like a runaway elephant.

"This year," he told his friend, Killebrew, "I either make it or quit dreaming and go back to Raytown and get a job."

"I have an idea you'll make it," Killebrew replied. "You hit well in Chattanooga last year."

Yes, he had hit well. It had been his first big year with the bat. In his previous three years in the minors, he had failed to hit more than .256. But last year he had zoomed to .307 and had driven in 93 runs.

"I think last year I found myself," he said to Killebrew. "I began thinking with the pitcher, and I also began to control my swing more. I wasn't going for the fences, just trying to meet the ball—but I still got twenty-eight doubles, nine triples and nine home runs."

Allison started hustling at bat and in the field, and before long he was putting together a rather impressive spring training. The better he played, the more convinced he became that he would go north with the Senators when they broke camp. But there were many baseball-wise men who didn't share his confidence. Cookie Lavagetto, who was planning definitely on an outfield of Sievers, Lemon and Pearson, liked Allison's determination but was still doubtful that the big broad-shouldered youth would ever make it against major league pitching.

"Right now he's 'way ahead of the rest of the players because he played winter ball," he said. "We'll wait and see what happens when the pitchers start bearing down."

Among the Washington sportswriters there was also skepticism.

"He's hitting fast balls now," said one of them. "Wait until the pitchers start curving him. Allison is too eager with the bat and will tie himself in knots."

Another snorted, "If he's so good, how come he couldn't win a job in the outfield at Almendares last winter? He wasn't hitting and they put him on the bench."

"He may go north," said another, "but he'll be back in the minors by the first of May."

Despite official and unofficial skepticism, there were two men in the Washington camp who were watching Allison with growing interest, and they didn't share in the pessimism. One was Calvin Griffith, president of the Senators, and the other was farm director Sherry Robertson.

"I frankly think Allison is going to make it," said Griffith, "and make it big."

"I dunno," said Lavagetto. "He's played five hundred and thirty professional games and has only hit twenty-eight homers."

"He'll hit," piped up Robertson. "I like that big kid. I like everything about him."

He was a big kid, all right. Bob Allison was now twenty-four years old, had attained a height of six feet four inches and weighed 220 pounds. He was powerfully built, with shoulders and a chest that strained at his uniform. Albie Pearson, who had been named Rookie of the Year in 1958, took one look at Allison and wiped his brow.

"Whew!" he said. "He's a big one. He can run, he can throw, and he swings that bat pretty good. I can see where I'm going to have to fight for my job."

Pearson was right. Allison gave him a battle for the center-field spot from the first day of training. Bob made every play at fever pitch. He never let up. He hit with gusto and fielded sensationally, and when he let go with throws from the outfield to home he almost tore the catcher's glove off.

"The kid's got an arm that fires like a gun," said one admirer.

It was Allison's arm, on one occasion, that got the Senators out of trouble and into trouble—on the same play. During a two-game series with the Kansas City Athletics in West Palm Beach, Allison had cut down two Kansas City runners with spectacular throws that brought the crowd to its feet. The throws helped the Senators stall off a couple of Kansas City rallies.

In the second game the Athletics had Hal Smith on third base with Hector Lopez at bat. Allison was playing right field and he backed up a few steps. He knew that Lopez was quite capable of giving the ball a long ride. Sure enough, Lopez lifted a high fly deep into right field and Allison waited near the fence for the catch. A quick glance told him that Smith was tagging up at third, ready to race home after the catch.

The ball came down and Bob gloved it. Almost with the same motion he uncorked a throw that brought a big "Ooh!" from the stands. It hopped on one bounce into the waiting mitt of catcher

Clint Courtney, and Smith, coming in, saw the big catcher waiting for him with the ball.

There was nothing to do but to barrel into Courtney and try to knock the ball out of his hand. Smith threw a football block on Courtney, but Courtney never faltered. He put the ball on Smith, rolled over in the dirt, but held onto the ball for the putout.

Only one thing went wrong. Courtney suffered a broken leg in the collison at the plate.

Later a couple of baseball writers were discussing the play.

"It might seem crazy to say it this way," said one of them, "but if that Allison's arm had been a little weaker, the play at the plate would have been closer. And if the play had been closer, Smith would have slid for the plate, and Courtney probably wouldn't have ended up with a broken leg!"

Throughout the spring training games Allison continued to excel in every facet of the game—and base running was another art at which he showed adeptness. In a Grapefruit League game with the Pittsburgh Pirates, Allison singled, and when the next batter hit a ground ball, he headed for second. Veteran shortstop Dick Groat came over to cover second base on the attempted double play. He got the ball ahead of Allison, all right, forcing him, but Allison was determined to break up the throw to first. He smashed into Groat like a runaway locomotive and knocked him spinning. Groat was shaking for several minutes afterwards.

"Man, how that kid runs!" said Sherry Robertson with delight. "When he goes from first to second, you can hear the ground rumble!"

"And when he slides, he's big enough to scare an infielder right out of his britches," said coach Ellis Clary.

It was this kind of aggressive play that made Allison a standout at Tinker Field in 1959. He went all-out all the time. He never relaxed. Every play was a crisis to him, and he treated every play in which he was involved as a personal test of his skill. To everyone in camp it became apparent that here was a young man with a determination that would not quit. And despite a few who were not convinced of his talents, it was generally felt that here was one of the most complete rookie ballplayers to invade the Florida training camps in years.

The impression left on his superiors stood Allison in good stead when cutdown time came before the team moved north. Calvin Griffith called manager Lavagetto and the coaches into his suite at the Cherry Plaza Hotel in Orlando. He had a list of minor league prospects, and the job was to determine which ones deserved to stick with the club. Carefully the group of men went over each man, evaluating his hitting, fielding, running and throwing. When Allison's name came up, coach Ellis Clary spoke up.

"There's a guy I'd like to see us keep," he said. "I'm not sure yet that he'll hit, but I know he'll scare the daylights out of the opposition. He's a hustler."

"He can field and run," conceded Lavagetto. "But I'm not sure about his hitting either."

"I like his attitude," said Griffith. "He gives you a hundred percent all the time. Let's keep him with the club and see if he can stick all year."

So Bob Allison was made a member of the Washington Senators and moved north as the team broke camp. With him went his friend Harmon Killebrew.

Bob Allison was certain that he could meet major league standards in fielding, throwing and base running. But he knew as well as anyone that he would have to hit with consistency to stay in the lineup. As the team neared the start of the regular season, it still looked as if Lavagetto would start Sievers, Lemon and Pearson in the outfield, and that Allison would have to be content on the bench until some circumstance occurred that would put him in the lineup.

In an effort to improve his hitting, he talked constantly with Roy Sievers. Sievers, who had a classic swing, was always happy to help, and he gave Allison much valuable advice.

"You're having trouble hitting breaking stuff," he said. "I'd suggest you stand a little closer to the plate. Keep your eye on the ball all the time, and when you get your pitch, have a good riffle at it. Some guys crouch at the plate, but I could always swing better from an upright position. Try that and I think you'll improve."

A little later Sievers advised Allison to use a heavier bat. Allison tossed aside his 34½-inch-long, 32-ounce bat and used one 36 inches long and 36 ounces in weight.

"You've been overswinging," Sievers said, "and you haven't been reaching outside pitches with the short bat. This ought to slow down your swing just enough so that you can connect with those."

"I'll probably strike out more with a heavier bat," said Allison doubtfully.

"Well, maybe you will," conceded Sievers. "But you'll get more hits too. One thing you have to learn—don't be impatient at the plate. You don't have to lunge toward the ball to hit it. It will come to you. Wait for it."

Bob Allison's dedication and anxiety to learn were not lost on President Calvin Griffith. One day, just before the start of the 1959 season, Griffith had a conference with Lavagetto.

"Cookie," he said carefully, "I don't think I've ever imposed on you before, but I want you to do me a personal favor."

"What is that?" Lavagetto asked.

"I want you to play Allison and Killebrew."

Lavagetto was shocked at the request. He had already set his mind on an outfield of Sievers, Lemon and Pearson.

"I doubt if either one can hit major league pitching," he said.

"I think they will," said Griffith. "Look, Cookie. I've seen more of those boys than you have. You've only seen them in spring training. I've studied them, got reports on them and know what makes them tick. They both have a lot of potential. Anyway, we've been in seventh or eighth place for four years. Frankly, I think it's time we make changes, try things, go out on a limb if we have to. Play Allison and Killebrew for one month and see what they do."

"Well, if you insist," said Lavagetto. "But I think they'll play themselves right out of the lineup."

"If they do," said Griffith, "I'll take all the raps."

It was a bold decision on Griffith's part. But he felt he was on firm ground. In Allison's case, he liked the young man's spirit and he liked the .307 batting average Bob had posted in Chattanooga in 1958. He even liked the nine home runs.

"Nine home runs in that park," he told a sportswriter, "are worth twenty-five anywhere else."

Opening day in Washington, D.C., is always something special, with either the President of the United States or the Vice-President tossing out the first ball from a flag-draped box. But 1959 was extra special because it was the 100th Anniversary of baseball in the nation's capital. One hundred years before, a group of government clerks had formed a baseball team called the Potomacs, and organized baseball in one form or another had existed in Washington, D.C., ever since.

There were more than 25,000 fans on hand when Vice-President Richard M. Nixon, in a relief role for President Eisenhower, threw out the first ball. A few minutes later right-hander Pedro Ramos strode to the mound to open the game against the Baltimore Orioles.

From a power standpoint, the Washington Senators were starting with an impressive outfield. Bob Allison had been assigned to right field where, hopefully, he would remain as one of the Senators' long-ball hitters. Jim Lemon was the cleanup man, and his ability to knock the ball out of the park was well known. Roy Sievers' capabilities in this direction were also recognized. This threesome gave the Senators an outfield capable, on paper at least, of doing great damage to American League pitching.

The infield consisted of Norm Zauchin at first, Reno Bertoia at second, Ron Samford at short and Harmon Killebrew at third. The catcher was Ed Fitzgerald and the crafty Ramos was on the hill for the opener.

And on the bench was little Albie Pearson, Rookie of the Year in 1958, who had correctly predicted that Allison would give him a fight for his job.

When the national anthem was finished, Bob Allison ran out on the field. He had butterflies in his stomach the same as the year before, when he had come up to the Senators for a brief, end-of-the-season trial. This time, though, Allison was in the starting lineup on opening day, and before him lay a long season in which he hoped to pin down definitely his place on the team. He stood in right field, watching Pedro Ramos take his pregame warm-ups, wondering if he would be able to help this team out of the doldrums. Four straight years in either seventh or eighth place was just too much!

Allison started to help in his first time at bat. Roy Sievers walked to open the second inning. Allison got the bunt signal from the bench and laid it down perfectly—so perfectly that he beat it out for his first 1959 hit. As Hoyt Wilhelm, the Baltimore pitcher, stretched for his pitch to Ed Fitzgerald, Allison took a generous lead off the bag. Sievers, now on second, also moved away from the keystone sack.

Fitzgerald hit the ball on a line and both runners broke. Then came sudden disaster. Fitzgerald's drive looked as if it would pass well over the head of Bob Boyd, the Oriole first baseman. But Boyd went high in the air, speared the ball, and fired it to Chico Carresquel covering second. Sievers was doubled off. Chico then whipped the ball back to Boyd in time to get Allison, who was desperately trying to scramble back to first base.

It was the first triple play ever executed on opening day by any major league club!

Allison went out to right field at the end of the inning feeling slightly dazed. But he recovered sufficiently to add another single to make it two-for-four for the day. Washington beat Baltimore, 9–2.

In the clubhouse, Allison was still shaking his head over the fast triple killing the Orioles had made.

"Do they always do things like that in the majors?" he asked Sievers with a grin.

"Not every day," said Sievers dryly.

6

Rain washed out the next two games for the Washington Senators, and Allison had time to reflect on his opening-day performance. He was pleased that he had managed two hits off Hoyt Wilhelm, the famous knuckleballer.

"That guy throws a pitch that flutters all over the place," he said to Killebrew. "He's tough."

"He certainly is," said Killebrew, modestly forgetting that he had hit Wilhelm for a homer in the game.

The second game of the 1959 season was played at Fenway Park in Boston. Allison and Killebrew were now roommates on the road, and they discussed hitting problems almost constantly. For both, this was the most critical year of their careers, and each valued any help he could get from the other.

"That close left-field wall is made to order for a right-handed hitter," Allison said hopefully at batting practice.

"The Boston pitchers will probably keep everything outside to us right-handers, though, to keep us from pullling the ball," said Killebrew.

Allison cleared the wall a couple of times in practice and went back to the bench just before game-time feeling an increasing confidence seep through him. He had a premonition that this was going to be a good year for him.

Allison didn't hit a homer over that left-field wall in the game, but he had a single in four times, stole a base and scored a run. It was in the sixth inning that Allison lashed his line-drive single to left center off Boston pitcher Ike Delock. Then he got a good lead off first, went down with the pitch, and thundered into the bag with a stolen base. Norm Zauchin then slapped a single to right and Allison romped home with a run.

It was a reasonably good day for Allison, but Washington lost the game, 7–3.

The following day Bob got another hit as Boston thumped the Senators again by the same score. Then, on April 16, the same two teams tangled at Fenway Park, and this game was a momentous one in Allison's budding career.

Herb Moford was on the mound for Boston, and for the first three innings he baffled the Washington batters completely. Meantime, the Red Sox picked up single runs in the second and third to lead the Senators, 2–0.

Albie Pearson, substituting for an injured Roy Sievers, opened the top of the fourth inning with a single. Ed Fitzgerald followed with another one-baser, putting two men on the bags.

It was Allison's turn to bat. He stepped gingerly into the batter's box and waved his bat threateningly at the pitcher. Moford had no "book" on Allison, didn't know his strengths or his weaknesses. Working slowly, the pitcher tried Allison with a curve on the outside corner. The umpire raised his right hand.

"Stee-rike!"

Moford went into his stretch, glanced at the base runners and delivered one outside. Ball one. Allison inched closer to the plate. Obviously, Moford was going to try to keep the ball on the outside edge so that the powerfully built Allison couldn't pull it over that inviting left-field wall.

Moford stretched, delivered. The ball was a breaking pitch,

but Allison timed it perfectly. He swung, and the crack of the
bat was music in his ear. The ball went up, up, up, as if it would
climb to the sky. It disappeared over the left-field wall for Bob
Allison's first major league homer—a three-run blast that put the
Senators ahead, 3–2!

It was the hit that sparked the Senators to victory. Norm
Zauchin added another homer in the same inning, and later Allison hit a single to make it two-for-four. Washington won, 7–5.

In the clubhouse everyone congratulated Allison on the first
home run of his major league career. And when Cookie Lavagetto slapped him on the seat of the pants and said, "Nice clout,
Bob," Allison felt that, at long last, he belonged on a major
league club.

Having now hit safely in each of his first four games, Allison
went out the next day and extended the streak to five with another single as the Baltimore Orioles won over Washington,
4–3. On April 18 Baltimore again won, 6–1, but Allison hit
another single to keep his hitting streak alive.

The next day the Orioles and Senators split a doubleheader,
Baltimore winning the first game, 7–5, and Washington grabbing
the nightcap, 4–2. In the first game Allison had three hits in five
times up and drove in two runs. In the second he got a single
out of four.

The following day the Senators met the New York Yankees
in Yankee Stadium. It was really no contest, with Don Larsen
beating the Senators, 11–4, but in the sixth inning Washington
managed to ignite a couple of firecrackers. Bob Allison clobbered his second major league home run off Larsen and Jim
Lemon duplicated the feat. It was the ninth straight game since
the beginning of the season in which Allison had hit safely!

But all streaks eventually some to an end, and Bob's did the
next day when New York edged Washington, 1–0, in fourteen
innings. Allison failed to get a hit in six times up.

Although Allison was personally enjoying a good start in his first full major league season, the club itself was in the midst of a desperate struggle. By April 30 the Senators had a record of seven wins and nine losses and were in fifth place. The team was hitting well enough, but the pitching was bad and the fielding highly questionable.

On a couple of occasions Allison added to the doubtfulness of the fielding. He was an excellent fly chaser, but it was his fine throwing arm that continued to get him and his team into trouble. It was too good.

Bob was justifiably proud of his ability to throw a ball as far as the best in the business, and maybe farther, and occasionally he would allow his enthusiasm for uncorking a throw get the better of his judgment. Often he would cut loose with a throw from the outfield that would reach the catcher without a bounce —even though there was no chance to get the runner. If there were trailing runners on the bags, they would move up into scoring position on Allison's unnecessary throw.

One day Cookie Lavagetto read the riot act to him.

"Look, Bob, you've got a great arm. You're capable of heaving a ball far enough to get a big roar from the crowd. But it doesn't always help the ball club. I want you to keep your throws down. Don't arch them high and far into the catcher's mitt. Throw them low, bullet-like, on a line. This will permit the throw to be cut off by an infielder if there is a chance to get another runner on the bases or keep him from advancing. Like I say, your arm is one of the best around, but you're going to have to learn to control it or it's going to cost us games."

Allison, as always, was willing to listen to reason.

"I guess I just didn't realize what I was doing with those throws, Cookie," he said. "I'll watch them."

And he did. Within a few days he was throwing low and hard to the infield and had conquered his natural desire to show off his arm with a long heave.

Criticism was also levied at Allison's base running. One coach said, "We're going to have to teach that kid to slide. He hits the ground two feet from the bag and knocks the infielder for a loop. Someday he's going to try that and the guy is going to get up and knock his block off!"

George Lentz, the Senator's trainer, laughed. "Well, I'll tell you something. I'd hate to be the guy who tries to knock Allison's block off. I've worked with a lot of athletes in my thirty-one years—including some big guys on the Washington Redskins —and I've never seen a guy stronger than Allison. There's just nobody to compare with him. I'll tell you, I'd hate to get him mad at me."

Early in May the Washington club traveled to Chicago to meet the White Sox. In the first game Allison hit his third home run of the season and helped the Senators defeat the Sox, 8–3.

In the second game, on May 6, the Senators' Camilo Pascual and Chicago's Early Wynn hooked up in a pitchers' duel. By the time the seventh inning rolled around the score was Chicago 3, Washington 2.

In the Washington half of the seventh, Faye Throneberry led off with a single to right field. Pascual, not a dangerous hitter, drew a walk when Wynn pitched him too carefully. Reno Bertoia then topped a pitch toward third base and beat it out for a hit.

The bases were loaded and Bob Allison was up.

Although the season was still young, news about Allison's better-than-average hitting was getting around among pitchers. In addition, Wynn didn't like the size of the big outfielder, the broadness of his shoulders or the thickness of his arms.

Wynn, a crafty pitcher with long experience, was determined not to give Allison anything too good. At the same time, he couldn't afford to walk him because it would force in the tying run.

Wynn worked the outside corner for a strike. Then he came in tight with another. Bob stepped out of the box, got dirt on his hands, and stepped back in. With a two-strike count, he would now have to swing at anything that looked good. Wynn knew he had the advantage now, that he could make Allison hit his own pitch.

Wynn stretched, glanced at the runners jockeying on the bases, and delivered a pitch outside by a hair. Allison wouldn't bite on it and the count was one-and-two.

"Strike the bum out!" roared a frog-voiced fan.

There's nothing Wynn wanted to do more. He tested Allison with another outside pitch, but again Bob ignored it. Two-and-two. Wynn went into his stretch again, cocked his leg and threw the ball. It came in over the heart of the plate, a fast ball with a tantalizing hop. Allison swung.

The shock of bat against ball radiated up Bob's arms. The sound of bat against ball had finality in it. And the flight of the ball looked magnificent as it sailed high and far into the left-field stands.

It was Bob Allison's first major league grand-slam homer!

Allison's clout made the score 6–3 in favor of the Senators and proved to be the winning margin as Washington beat Chicago by a final score of 6–4.

In the clubhouse there were congratulations again, and a sportswriter came up to Allison and asked the obvious question. "How did it feel, getting that grand-slam homer off Early Wynn?"

Allison grinned happily. "How about that? It's the first time I ever hit a homer off a forty-thousand-dollar-a-year pitcher!"

While all of this was going on, the Senators as a team began to win, mostly on the heavy hitting of Allison, Killebrew, Lemon and Sievers. This foursome was now firmly established as a most effective "Murderers' Row." It had been a long time since Senator fans had seen such clouting, and pitchers all over the league were discussing ways and means of stopping the Washington hitters.

"Allison and Killebrew are two of the strongest guys in the league," one of them said. "I swear they could be holding back on a swing and still knock it into the stands."

"And don't forget Lemon and Sievers," said another. "If one doesn't get you, the other will."

On May 9 the hit-happy Senators moved into Yankee Stadium to take on the Bronx Bombers. Aware of the new power in the Washington lineup, the Yankees went with their pitching ace, Bob Turley. But on this day, at least, he was no match for the Senators. Allison clouted another home run and Killebrew had two. Hal Griggs pitched a two-hit shutout for the Washington club as the Senators won, 9–0.

Allison was now hitting .293, had four home runs, and had batted in seventeen. And the Senators, surprising everyone in the league, had risen to third place with fourteen wins and eleven losses. But the Yanks took some of the pleasure out of the situation by dumping the Senators twice the following day, 6–3 and 3–2.

A few days later the Senators met the Cleveland Indians, and this turned out to be a game in which Bob's prodigious strength came in handy again. During the game a bit of "bad blood" developed between the two teams. Pedro Ramos was on the mound for the Senators and some of his pitches were coming in too close to Cleveland batters for their comfort. Joe Gordon, manager of the Indians, had some words with Ramos. A couple of players jawed back and forth. And suddenly—much to Allison's surprise, since he was peacefully patrolling center field at the time—several skirmishes erupted on the infield.

Players poured from each dugout, and within seconds several fights were going on. Allison raced in from the outfield. He wasn't by nature a belligerent person, and his intention was to stop some of the fighting.

As he neared the infield he saw Cleveland catcher Russ Nixon pinning a Washington player to the ground. Allison rushed forward, wrapped his arms around Nixon and pulled him off the fallen Washington player.

Much to everyone's surprise, particularly Nixon's, Bob tore

off the catcher's chest protector and shirt as he lifted him off his feet. The action was so funny it practically stopped the entire scuffle. Nixon walked red-faced and bare-chested to the dugout to get dressed again.

Later, in the clubhouse, Allison shrugged his shoulders when a reporter asked him about his part in the melee.

"I just saw Nixon on top of one of our guys and wanted to pull him off," said Allison simply. "I didn't know his shirt and chest protector were going to come off in my hands."

Trainer George Lentz, who had known all the time what a tremendous physical specimen Bob was, just grinned from ear to ear.

"I told you I'd never want to mix with him," he said.

About mid-May the Detroit Tigers arrived in Washington to do battle with the "new look" Senators. Frank Lary, ace of the Tiger pitching staff, was selected to stop the Washington club's hostile sluggers. And for five innings he did just that. He had the Senators eating out of his hand, baffling them with an assortment of curves, fast balls and sliders. The Tigers were ahead, 3–0. In the last of the sixth Albie Pearson, playing right field that day, singled. Allison stepped in to face the crafty Lary.

Lary worked on him methodically, but it did him little good. Allison ripped a double off the left-center-field wall to score Pearson from first and break the ice for the Senators. A moment later Allison scored on a Killebrew homer and the score was deadlocked. The Senators went on to win, 7–4.

Detroit defeated Washington the following day, 4–2, although Allison collected his seventh homer of the season. Against the Kansas City A's the next day the Senators won, 7–2. Pascual had a no-hitter going until the eighth inning when Bob Cerv spoiled it with a double, and the Athletics went on to score two in the ninth to also spoil the shutout. But Allison had two-for-four in the game, including his eighth home run of the year.

Later in May an exciting game occurred with the Boston Red

Sox at Fenway Park. Allison clouted a homer over the always-beckoning wall in the fourth to put Washington ahead, 1–0, but the game seesawed back and forth, and at the end of the nine innings it was tied 4–4. Neither team scored in the tenth, but in the eleventh Washington erupted.

Allison opened the inning with a sharp single off Murray Wall. Killebrew then drove a one-bounce single to Ted Williams in left field. Allison wheeled around second and headed for third, but Williams' throw cut him down. Then came the deluge. Jim Lemon homered, Julio Becquer doubled, Faye Throneberry doubled, Ron Samford walked, Ed Fitzgerald doubled, Truman Clevenger sacrificed, Reno Bertoia singled, and Allison, up for the second time in the inning, struck out to end the slaughter. Washington had scored six times to put the game away, 10–4.

It was nearing the end of May now, and Allison was proving that he had staying power. He was hitting .290, with nine home runs and twenty-eight RBI's. There was no longer any doubt that Calvin Griffith's decision to play Allison regularly had been the right one. By this time Cookie Lavagetto was firmly entrenched on Allison's side.

"He's a great kid," Lavagetto said to a sportswriter one day. "If he makes a mistake, he won't sulk or try to hide it. He comes right out and talks about it. He wants to learn and he does learn. I've never seen him make the same mistake twice. As for hitting, Bob studies the pitchers. I've seen him sit in the dugout before a game, analyzing the opposing starter all by himself. He'll sit there and mutter, 'This guy uses fast balls only occasionally. But he's got a neat slow curve and a slider. That's what I'm going to have to watch for.'"

"What about his fielding?" asked the writer.

"Tops," said Lavagetto. "Allison studies fielding problems the same way he studies hitting. The guy is never satisfied with his performance. He has practically a mania to excel at everything. Some players, when they fail to hit, are lousy in the field. Not Bob. If anything, he works harder to make up for a bad day at bat. He wants to be the most complete ballplayer to come along in years—and that's just about what he is."

The Washington Senators' confidence in Bob Allison's ability to do the job for them was verified publicly on May 27. On that day Calvin Griffith traded Albie Pearson, Rookie of the Year in 1958, to the Baltimore Orioles. The move cemented Allison's grip on an outfield job for 1959.

7

By the first week in June, Bob Allison had raised his batting average to a lusty .303 and had collected twelve home runs and thirty-three RBI's. By now he was a local hero to the long-suffering Washington fans. The downtrodden Senators had lacked color for so long that fans didn't know quite what to make of the four super-sluggers now in the lineup. Having a ball club that could score runs, and score them dramatically, fascinated the Washington followers. It had been a long dry spell, and they were now eager to take to their hearts anyone who could create a little excitement in old Griffith Stadium.

Allison emerged as a sort of matinee idol. He was not only big and powerful, but ruggedly handsome at the same time. He had hazel eyes, long lashes, wavy hair, and a genuine friendliness toward fans demanding autographs. In other words, he had the look of a hero. It was noticed, after a while, that afternoon games played on weekdays drew many women to the ball park—most of them eager to see Bob Allison. Women admired him for his physical prowess; men had admiration for him as a ballplayer.

Despite the Senators' heavy hitting and the excitement this generated among the fans, the strange truth was that Washington was an ineffective ball club in 1959. Power was their long suit, and they could give bad dreams to any pitcher in the league. But they had little else. Their pitching was spotty and their fielding below average, and it was evident to Lavagetto that hitting alone couldn't take them very high in the final league standings. On June 1 the Senators were treading water in seventh place with twenty-one wins and twenty-six losses, and prospects of their improving their won-lost record seemed remote.

But Bob Allison's personal record was something else, and on June 9 he posted another memorable game in his new career. The Senators were entertaining the Chicago White Sox in Washington. Chicago scored a run in the top half of the first inning. Facing Bob Shaw, Allison came up in the bottom half of the same inning with the bases empty and drilled one into the left-field stands to tie the score, 1–1. In the fourth Chicago scored another run, which was promptly matched by Washington in their half.

Battling to stay ahead, Chicago scored two runs in the top of the seventh to make the score Chicago 4, Washington 2. In the bottom half of the inning, Allison found himself at bat with a runner on base.

Shaw bore down on Allison. Bob fouled one off. A pitch came in wide. Another was tight and high, driving Allison away from the plate. Two balls and one strike.

Allison looked for a fast ball and got it. He drove it high and far into the seats for his second home run, tying the game again, 4–4. In the last half of the eighth the Washington team scored three more to put the game on ice—but it had been Allison's two homers that had kept them in the game until they could break loose with the clinching rally.

It was Allison's first two-homer game in the majors.

Bob continued to hit well during the month of June. His speed in the outfield, his throwing and his hitting stamped him as one of the best rookies to crash the American League in many years. On June 17 he hit another homer for Washington, and this one was the eightieth hit by the Senators during the season. Washington was leading the league in home runs—but running seventh in the standings!

And the big rookie from Raytown was fourth in the league in homers, behind Killebrew, Rocky Colavito and Gus Triandos, all with more experience than he had.

But despite Allison's serious approach to the game, there were moments of lightness too. One day when the Senators' game was being telecast, a brief shower delayed the start of the game. The Washington players sat in the dugout waiting for the rain to stop, and it was during this kind of off-moment that Washington players would often kid Allison about his great strength. This time it was Pedro Ramos, the Cuban pitcher, who felt in a teasing frame of mind. He would run up behind Allison, slap him on the back of the neck, and then run out of danger.

None of the players knew that the TV cameras, seeking to entertain viewers while the rains fell, were focused on the Washington dugout, catching this bit of byplay. Each time Ramos slapped Allison, Bob would whirl around to catch him, but the fleet-footed Cuban would dash out of reach. Finally, Allison caught him. He grabbed Ramos around the middle, pinning both arms with his own forearm. Ramos started squirming, but even though the blood rushed to the excited Cuban's face, he could not break Allison's bear-like hug.

TV viewers could plainly see what Allison was saying to the wriggling Ramos.

"Say uncle!" he kept demanding. "Say uncle!"

Ramos puffed and squirmed.

"Say uncle!" Allison repeated, tightening his grip.

Finally Ramos could stand no more of it. In his Cuban accent he screamed, "Hokay, hokay! Oncle, oncle!"

In the TV booth one of the announcers grinned and said, "Allison has just made his wrestling debut on TV."

The last ten days of June saw Allison pounding the ball with as much power as he had displayed in subduing Ramos. In Detroit one night he got three-for-four—a double and two singles—off Frank Lary. The next day Washington whipped the Tigers twice, 4–3 and 7–5, and Alison's second-game homer helped to decide that one. A few nights later Washington beat Kansas City, 8–4, with a barrage of four homers by Allison, Lemon, Killebrew and Throneberry.

By the first of July the Senators had managed to climb to sixth place with a won-lost record of 33-39. The Cleveland Indians were leading the league.

Washington paid a call at Yankee Stadium for the big July 4 doubleheader that year. The first game was a slugging match, and Allison collected three-for-five, including a double. Washington won, 10–6.

But there was a bigger thrill in store for Allison that day than battering Yankee pitchers for three hits. In the clubhouse between games he received the news that his wife had given birth to a new son, who would be named William Kirk.

"Congratulations!" said Killebrew. "That's great!"

The other players crowded around, congratulating the new father.

"You oughta have a good second game in honor of the new baby," somebody said.

"I'm going to try," said Allison.

It would be nice to report that an inspired Allison clobbered Yankee pitching to a fare-thee-well. But he didn't. He went hitless in the second game, which New York won, 7–0.

"Guess I was too excited," he said afterward.

Nevertheless, Allison was now hitting .290, with twenty-one home runs and fifty-two RBI's to his credit. His record had Casey Stengel, manager of the Yankees, shaking his head.

"Me, I got a left-field problem," he moaned. "We had a chance to get that Allison fellah, but we didn't get him. He could solve my problem in left field if I had him."

When told of the remark, Allison just grinned. "It's nice to know that Casey thinks well of me," he said, "but I believe I made the right decision coming to Washington. You know, I only hit .256, .233, .246 and .307 in my minor league seasons, but Washington went along with me and brought me up. I doubt if the Yankees would have stuck with me the way Calvin Griffith did."

Probably because Allison was a rookie, he was not selected for the first All-Star Game in 1959. But he was later picked as a utility man by Casey Stengel, who was managing the American Leaguers. Casey was flying to Pittsburgh for the game when he learned that Al Kaline, star outfielder for the Tigers, might not be able to make the game because of a fractured cheekbone. The Washington group on the plane tossed Allison's name in Casey's lap as a replacement.

"You know," said Casey, "that ain't a bad idea. That big guy might help us."

Although Kaline made the game after all, Bob was chosen by Casey to fill out the squad. Bob did not play but maybe he should have, because the National League edged the American League in a squeaker, 5–4.

The first game for the Senators after the All-Star break was with the Baltimore Orioles at Washington. Again the hard-hitting Senators went on a home-run rampage, with Allison, Killebrew, Sievers and Ken Aspromonte hitting round-trippers.

The next day was Allison's twenty-fifth birthday, and Bob made the most of it. In the bottom half of the first inning he singled with the bases empty. Killebrew brought him around with a homer. In the fifth the same two sluggers combined hits to produce another run. This time Allison hit a long triple off Hal Brown and Killebrew singled him home. Washington eventually won the game, 9–3.

A few days later, Washington batters got only five hits off Tiger pitching, but Allison managed two of them—his twenty-third homer and a single—and paced the Senators to a 4–2 win. On another occasion Frank Lary, the Tiger ace, held Washington to four hits, and Bob got two of them, a homer and a single. Allison was managing to get his hits even though the team slipped.

On July 28 the Senators arrived in Kansas City for a series. Allison found his family and all of his friends from Raytown on hand to greet him. It was "Allison Night" in Kansas City's Municipal Stadium, and among the gifts he received was a scholarship at the University of Kansas which would permit him to complete his college work.

But even more unusual was the fact that the Washington players chipped in money to buy Allison gifts of their own. They presented him with an air conditioner and a radio.

"That's pretty nice," commented one sportswriter. "The kid is real popular with his teammates. How many times have you seen a rookie get gifts from his teammates, anyway?"

"I'd have to say never," said another reporter.

By the end of July, Allison's batting average of .286 was the highest on the club. He had twenty-six homers and had driven in sixty-two runs.

All this was fine for Allison, but strangely it didn't do the Senators much good. The team continued to lose, and in one horrifying stretch they lost eighteen straight games! This tumbled them into last place and mired them there.

When the second All-Star Game of the year was played, Bob Allison found himself selected to the squad, along with Killebrew, Sievers and Ramos. Unfortunately, he didn't get to play

—but the very fact of being selected in his first major league season was honor enough for Allison. This time the American League won, 5–3.

Along with his hitting, Allison was excelling in other facets of the game. His base running, for example, was giving opposing players fits. In a game played August 16 at Baltimore, Allison gave an example of aggressive base running that raised some hairs on the top of Baltimore shortstop Billy Klaus' head.

Up in the first inning, Bob singled to left. Julio Becquer also singled and Allison, in a burst of speed, fell going around second. Seeing Allison sprawled on the ground, the Baltimore outfielder whipped the ball to shortstop Klaus. Allison, just struggling to his feet, should have been an easy out. Instead, he slid hard into second base, kicked the ball out of Klaus' hand and was called safe.

On August 19 Allison hit his twenty-eighth home run of the season at Cleveland. On August 30 he hit his twenty-ninth round-tripper. This started Calvin Griffith to buzzing.

"Ted Williams holds the American League record for the most home runs in a rookie year—thirty-one," he said. "It looks as if Bob will be able to break Williams' mark. He's got twenty-nine already and there's a month to go."

By this time, of course, Griffith was walking on air anyway. His gamble with both Allison and Killebrew had paid off. Killebrew had more homers than Allison, but he was hitting for a lower average. Since Killebrew had spent two years on the Washington bench as a bonus baby, he was not considered a rookie in 1959. Allison was, and for this reason his performance was all the more remarkable.

"That boy's got a chance to break Williams' record," Griffith kept saying.

The speculation served to put Allison squarely on the spot. He wanted desperately to live up to the expectations Griffith had for him. He wanted to beat Williams' record more than anything in the world. But the pressure built, game after game,

and Bob tightened up. In the first week of September he went
into a batting slump, the first serious one he had suffered all
year. On September 5 Lavagetto benched him, then put him
back in the next day after the rest. Allison went hitless. He
played a few more days and failed to deliver at the plate, and
on September 10 he was benched again. That benching lasted
four days.

Griffith was close to tearing out his hair.

"He's got to do it!" he exclaimed. "He's still got two weeks."

Allison returned to the lineup on September 14 and went
nothing-for-four. It was not until September 23 that he connected for his thirtieth homer.

"He's still got over a week to hit two more," said Griffith
hopefully.

But Allison didn't make it. He ended the season with thirty
homers, one short of tying Ted Williams' rookie record, and
two short of breaking it. And to discourage Calvin Griffith just
a bit more, the Senators finished in last place.

But although Griffith was chagrined at the Senators' lowly
finish, he was even more disappointed in Allison. He had
wanted to proudly boast about his new find beating Williams'
record, but it hadn't happened. Still, Griffith and everyone
else had to admit that there was really nothing very disap-
pointing about Bob Allison's showing in 1959.

First of all, there was something special about Bob's thirty
home runs. As a right-handed batter, he faced few left-handed
pitchers, mainly because most of the other Senators also were
right-handed. But that meant nothing to Allison—twenty-nine
of his thirty homers were hit off right-handed hurlers! He
homered in every park except Baltimore, and twenty-one of his
thirty homers were made against first-division teams. He also
proved to be the team's best clutch hitter, with seventeen of his
homers coming in tense situations after the sixth inning!

In addition to his talent for hitting round-trippers, Allison
posted a few more records. He led the American League in

triples with 9; finished fourth in total bases with 275, trailing only Rocky Colavito, Mickey Mantle and Harvey Kuenn; finished fourth in the league in homers; finished fifth in the league in stolen bases with 13, behind only Luis Aparicio, Mantle, Jim Landis and Jackie Jensen; ended in tenth place in RBI's with 85, although he was used in the No. 2 spot in the batting order for much of the season.

The young man from Raytown, Missouri—who had bounced around in the minor leagues posting unimpressive records for four years—had taken the American League by storm!

8

Bob Allison returned home in the fall of 1959 in high spirits. He was naturally delighted at the success he had enjoyed in his first year in the major leagues. So were his family, friends and neighbors. Everyone felt Bob had a great career ahead of him in the big-time, and he was inclined to admit as much to himself, if not to others.

But Bob Allison was not an idealist. He knew that one good year did not make a career. He considered carefully both his minor and major league record, weighed the pros and cons, totaled up the score—and came to a decision.

"We're going back to Cuba to play winter ball again," he announced to his wife.

"Do you think you have to this year?" Betty asked.

Bob nodded. "You can never get too good at baseball. I'm sure it will help me if I play winter ball again."

Before long, Allison was back with Almendares in the Cuban League, playing baseball in Fidel Castro's "new" country. One evening as he lounged in his Havana hotel room, the telephone rang. It was long distance from Kansas City.

"This is Merle Harmon, sportscaster for Station WDAF," said a friendly voice. "I've got good news for you."

"Hi, Merle," said Allison. "What's the news?"

"The Baseball Writers Association has just selected you as Rookie of the Year for 1959," Merle said.

Bob Allison was quiet for a moment.

"What do you think of that, Bob?" Merle pressed.

Allison finally found his voice. "Well, I guess I'm kind of speechless," he said slowly. "It's a real honor, I'll say that."

"You got eighteen of the twenty-four votes," Merle went on. "Did you have any idea that you might be chosen the year's best rookie?"

"Well, it did cross my mind a couple of times," Allison admitted truthfully. "Toward the end of the year I kind of figured it was an outside possibility. But then when I slumped in September, I figured that killed my chances."

"Your family has been notified, and half of Raytown knows it now," Merle said. "Your mother and father are pretty proud. How do you feel about it?"

"Well, as I say, it's an honor and I'll try hard to live up to it."

"Did you set any particular goals for yourself when the 1959 season started?" Merle wanted to know.

"Well, more or less. I concentrated on hitting the ball every time I went to the plate. I had no idea about hitting homers, I just wanted to hit safely. The homers began to come, though, and I guess toward the end of the season I was concentrating too much on hitting them. There was Williams' record to beat, and I knew Calvin Griffith wanted me to beat it, and I tried hard. I guess it was because I kept going for the fences that my average fell off in September."

"How do you account for becoming a power hitter in the majors when you didn't show that promise in the minors?"

"I can't really explain it," Allison said candidly. "I guess I just had more experience and confidence, and I also studied the pitchers more in the big leagues."

"What about 1960?"

Allison laughed. "I'm trying not to think of the sophomore jinx," he said.

"How's Almendares doing?" Merle asked.

"About the same as Washington. We're in last place too. When we hit, we don't get the pitching. When we get the pitching, we don't hit."

"Thanks, Bob," said Merle, closing the conversation, "and the best of luck next year."

"Thanks," said Allison. "I'm going to try to have a better year for the Senators next season."

Despite the Senators' bleak 1959 season, Cookie Lavagetto was signed to manage the club again in 1960. This move on Calvin Griffith's part amounted to a vote of confidence for the luckless manager, but it did not indicate complete satisfaction with the team's performance. Griffith was determined to improve the club, and what he wanted most of all was a good catcher to handle the Washington pitching staff.

When Bob Allison reported to Tinker Field in Orlando for spring training, there was more than trade talk in the air. There were still rumors floating around that the Washington Senators were on the verge of moving to Minneapolis. Bob had no particular preference, one way or another. He had enjoyed a fine season in 1959, and he saw no reason why he couldn't repeat in 1960, whether he played in Washington or Minneapolis.

Allison went to work with his usual eagerness at Orlando and had a highly successful spring training. The late-season slump in 1959 did not endure, and Bob began rapping the ball around in the Grapefruit League as if he owned the pitchers. He posted seven homers during the spring exhibition schedule and reaffirmed without question his position as a starter in the Senators' lineup. No longer were there cynical remarks about whether or not he could hit major league pitching.

Two weeks before the opening game of the season, Griffith, who had been busy on the telephone for months, finally obtained the catcher he was seeking. Earl Battey was acquired from the Chicago White Sox, but the Senators had to give up a good man to get him. That good man was Roy Sievers, one of the team's potent sluggers.

"We hated to let Roy go," Griffith said, "but it was a calculated risk. We got Battey to shore up our front-line catching, and we got Don Mincher too, a good prospect. We figured we could spare some of our power because we still have some pretty good hitters left on this club."

Despite rumors of a pending franchise shift to Minneapolis, the Senators opened the season against the Boston Red Sox at their old stamping grounds in Washington. The Washington lineup was again strong on power and weak on pitching and fielding. The three major sluggers were Bob Allison, who started in right field, Harmon Killebrew at third and Jim Lemon in left. In addition to these stalwarts, there was Billy Gardner at second, Len Green in center, Don Mincher at first, Earl Battey behind the plate, Billy Consolo at shortstop and, scheduled for the opener, the indomitable Camilo Pascual.

The day before the opener Lavagetto called a workout. It was a hot sultry day, even by Washington standards, and by the time the practice session was completed, Bob Allison was soaked with perspiration. He was one of the first to reach the clubhouse, and he stripped off his uniform quickly and padded toward the showers. As he entered the tiled cubicle he gave the hot water control a sharp twist—sharper than he had intended.

It was a bad mistake. In an instant the hot water, like red-hot needles, slashed down his left side, scalding him severely. Allison let out a cry of pain that echoed through the almost empty clubhouse. He stumbled out of the shower and into the training room.

Clinging desperately to George Lentz, the trainer, Allison made his way to the rubbing table. In an agony of pain, he lifted himself onto the table. Lentz looked at Allison's seared body and shook his head. Bob had suffered severe burns down his left side and thigh.

By this time, players had drifted in to see what had happened, and were gathered anxiously around the rubbing table.

"We heard that scream clear out in the dugout," one of them said.

"What happened anyway?" Lavagetto demanded.

"He's pretty badly burned," said Lentz, explaining what had occurred. "I doubt if—"

"I want to play tomorrow," said Allison quickly, gritting his teeth against the pain.

Lentz didn't answer. He went to work treating the injuries with a cooling salve, bandaging the most severe burns.

"I don't want this to keep me out of the lineup," Allison said again. "I can play."

Lavagetto looked doubtful. He admired Allison's grit, but the injuries seemed too grave to put him in the lineup.

"Every time you swing the bat it'll hurt," said Lentz. "In fact, every time you *move* it'll hurt."

Allison looked pleadingly at Lavagetto. "I want to start tomorrow," he said. "I can play. I guarantee you I can play. These burns—they look worse than they are."

Lavagetto shook his head uncertainly.

"We'll see how you feel tomorrow," he said.

Allison spent an almost sleepless night. He lay all night on his right side and even the weight of the blanket over him was a form of torture. He woke and dozed and woke again, and the pain was always there, but the next morning he was up and ready to go. When he showed up at the ballpark, Lavagetto approached him with concern on his face.

"How you feeling, Bob?" he asked.

"Not bad," said Allison. "I can start today. I really can."

Allison's appeal was so convincing that Lavagetto wrote his name in the starting lineup.

"But the minute you think it's too much for you, let me know," he said. "And if *I* think it's too much for you, I'll yank you out."

"Fair enough," said Bob.

Heavily bandaged, Allison appeared on the field and lined up with his teammates in front of President Dwight Eisenhower's box to retrieve his throw in pregame ceremonies. The President, beaming his wide smile, threw out the ball. Allison grabbed it and raced to the clubhouse to put the ball among his souvenirs.

The effort convinced him that Lentz was right—every move he made hurt. But when the umpire called "Play ball!" Bob Allison was in right field despite the excruciating pain that ravished the left side of his body.

Neither Boston nor Washington scored in the first inning, but the Red Sox tallied a run in the top of the second. In the bottom of the same inning Allison came to bat. He grounded out, and promptly learned another lesson about his injuries. A raw, searing pain racked his body as he swung at the pitch, and running to first required an almost superhuman effort.

Jim Lemon hit a homer with two on in that inning and the Senators had a 3-1 lead. The score was still 3-1 when the Washington fifth opened. Allison was the first hitter to face the Boston hurler, Al Worthington.

Allison ignored the first pitch, outside. The second was in tight and Bob swung, fouling it back. The pain down his left side came again and Allison sucked in his breath.

The third pitch was wide again, but the next one was over. Allison swung. The pain blistered him agonizingly. But ball and bat collided and the ball landed 375 feet away in the left-field stands for a home run!

Allison trotted slowly around the bases. Each step tormented him. He gritted his teeth and said to himself, *I can stay in. I can go another inning.*

All through the game he kept urging himself to stay in the lineup. The savage pain enveloped him when he ran in the outfield, when he reached up his arms to take a fly ball, when he threw the ball back to the infield, when he swung the bat. It even hurt while he sat on the bench. And each inning he would say to himself, *Just one more inning. Just one more.*

In the dugout Lavagetto sauntered over one time and asked Allison if he didn't want to be taken out.

"No. I want to play," Allison insisted.

He got through the sixth and seventh innings, and though he was in constant pain, he wouldn't quit. In the eighth inning he connected for a double, and this hit had to be run out despite his injuries. When the game ended he had two hits in four times at bat, a homer and a double. Pascual, in one of his finer games, had struck out fifteen men to establish a club record and Washington won, 10–1.

When the game was over, Allison walked slowly back to the clubhouse and collapsed wearily on a stool.

"Well, I made it," he said to Killebrew.

"What a guy!" Lentz said to Lavagetto. "A big tough kid."

Bob Allison went home and endured another pain-filled night during which he slept fitfully, but the next day he was ready to go again.

Very much concerned, his wife said, "Maybe you ought to let Cookie rest you a few days."

Allison shook his head. "I'm a starter, and I want to remain a starter. I don't want to go back to the bench. I can play."

And Allison did play. For a full week the pain was with him, tormenting him with every movement of arms, legs or body. But despite the handicap the injury placed on him, Allison not only remained in the lineup but posted one of the most remarkable weeks of his career!

In the second game of the new season, Allison stroked two hits in four times up, although Boston beat the Senators, 3–2. The next day Bob got three-for-four, and the day after that he had a double and a single in five tries. In the fifth game of the season Allison went four-for-five, and the newspapers began to talk about the fantastic pace of his hitting, despite severe injury.

Allison was batting .591!

The pace didn't slacken. On April 23 Allison had a single and double out of four. He was not only clouting the ball to all fields, but many of his hits came in critical situations.

On April 24, for example, Washington met the Boston Red Sox in a game that turned out to be a slugger's delight. In the eighth inning the score was tied, 7–7, and a parade of pitchers had walked to the mound on both sides.

Tom Sturdivant was serving them up for Boston when the eighth got under way. Billy Gardner, first up for the Senators, doubled to right center. This brought up Allison with a chance to break the tie.

Sturdivant worked cagily on the Washington slugger. He tested him with a curve outside, but Allison let it go. The next one was over the plate, low. Sturdivant was doing his best to keep Allison from lifting one out of the park.

With a one-one count, Sturdivant went to his fast ball. Bob swung. The ball screamed on a line into left center. It dropped in for a double and sent Gardner racing home with the go-ahead run. The hit set the stage for a four-run rally that proved to be just enough to win. The final score was Washington 11, Boston 10.

It was not until April 25, in the seventh game of the season, that Allison failed to hit. Milt Pappas of the Baltimore Orioles finally held him hitless in a 3–2 Oriole win.

But Allison, hampered by an injury that only now was beginning to subside, had hit an even .500 during the first seven games!

Washington moved into New York for a series with the Yankees, and before the opening game a sportswriter asked Allison about his injury.

"The burns are healing now," he said. "I feel fine."

Later, in the press box, the writer remarked to another reporter, "Allison's feeling better. He'll probably hit a thousand from now on."

Actually, Allison had only one-for-four that day, but it was an important hit. New York was leading, 4–1, when the top of the eighth opened. Whitey Ford was coasting along nicely for the Yanks, and it looked as if Washington was doomed to defeat.

Billy Gardner was first up in the eighth. He promptly laid down a bunt and beat it out for a hit. Dan Dobbeck, playing in center for Washington that day, was next up. He singled over second base, and Gardner went to third. Allison was up with men on first and third.

Whitey Ford, of course, was not unaware of the reckless manner in which Allison was hammering baseballs around American League parks, and he pitched to Bob with extreme care. He put a little something extra on his fast ball, and Allison fouled off two of them. A curve just missed the outside corner, another was in too close. Two and two.

The next pitch, another fast ball, came in a little higher than Whitey wanted. Allison drove it on a line into center to score Gardner and move Dobbeck to second.

Big Jim Lemon then came up and drove the ball into the stands to put Washington ahead, 5–4. That was the final score.

Naturally, Allison's early-season success pleased him. His big 1959 season was still a pleasant memory to him, and things seemed to be falling in line for him again in 1960. Still, he was smart enough to know that it was possible for things to change.

One day a Washington writer was asking him about his heavy and timely hitting.

"You know," Allison said analytically, "I still have a lot to learn. When you think you know it all, you always find out there's something you should have done better. The only way to play this game is all-out all the time. Then at least you know you've tried your best."

But Bob Allison would not have been human if he had not seen in his 1960 success a happy continuation of 1959. He was hitting the ball and giving American League pitchers fits, and even though he was aware that things could change, he could think of no really valid reason why they should. He was eager, he wanted to learn, and as he learned he would get even better—this seemed to be the direction things were taking.

But it is at times like these that a player's game sometimes begins to fall apart—and this happened to Allison. After his early-season splurge, he began to taper off. The hits did not fall in as readily, and the home run, his ace in the hole, did not come as frequently as he would have liked. As a result, Bob began to press a little.

One day in New York, Casey Stengel, who secretly admired the big Washington outfielder, made a casual comment. "You know, that big feller is gonna be one of the greatest hitters. Only he's got to learn something first. He's too eager up there at that plate. He gives in to the pitcher. I mean, he won't wait for that good pitch; he'll hit what the pitcher wants him to hit. So he swings at bad balls and things. I kinda hate to think what will happen when that big guy learns to swing at only the good ones."

Stengel had hit upon one of Allison's problems, and Bob was the first to admit it.

"Maybe I am too eager," he said to Killebrew. "I'm swinging at a lot of bad balls lately."

"I do the same thing," said Killebrew. "But it's a habit we should try to break. A good hitter waits for the right pitch."

"Some say I should cut down on my swing," said Allison, trying to analyze his situation. "But I don't know if I could do that. I know I shouldn't lunge at the ball—although I do it sometimes. I think everyone should have a nice, easy natural swing and stay with it. Let the ball fall where it will. As for home runs, they'll come if you have any power at all. You see, I know this, but I don't always put it into practice."

Both Allison and Killebrew had a strong urge to be superior ballplayers, but they were of different temperaments and they reacted differently to success and failure. Although Killebrew was serious about his career, he was not one to worry about his mistakes or to cry over spilled ball games. Allison, however, was a worrier. He worried about his slumps, his fielding lapses, the games the Senators lost, especially one-run losses which might have been wins *if* he had done this instead of that or had produced a hit instead of a fly ball in a critical situation.

"Don't take it to bed with you," Killebrew said once. "When the game's over, it's over. All you can do is try to do better the next day."

One day in mid-May, Allison hammered a triple to deep left center field, and as he ran it out he was aware of a pain in his stomach. When he reached third he called time. Lavagetto came from the dugout to see what was wrong.

"My stomach's upset," said Allison. "I feel sick."

Lavagetto put in a pinch runner for Allison and took the big slugger to the clubhouse. The next day Bob did not play, but the upset did not prove serious.

As the season went along, Allison found that he was not hitting with quite the consistency he had enjoyed in 1959. But he hit reasonably well and produced a fair quota of home runs

and clutch hits. For many players the season Allison was putting together would have been an excellent one indeed, but
for Bob it was below par. It was simply not up to the high
standards he had set in 1959 and hoped to maintain in 1960—
and it worried him.

On several occasions, as the season rolled along, Allison was
forced to call time, trot in from his right-field position, and report that his stomach was acting up. He was examined by the
club physician, Dr. George Resta, a number of times.

"I don't think there's anything basically wrong with Bob,"
the doctor said. "He's a big strong healthy guy. But he's got a
nervous stomach. Every play is a crisis for Allison, whether he
or somebody else is making it. He's tense all the time, on edge
all the time. It's simply an athletic stomach, a nervous condi-
tion, and Bob has it because of a desire to excel at the game
that's so strong that it worries him sick if he doesn't do as well
as he thinks he should."

All through the season Bob Allison worried about his re-
curring illness and the fact that he was not having the big year
he had expected. Still, when the final figures on the year were
posted, they were not too alarming. Allison batted .251 in 1960
as compared to .261 in 1959, he had 15 home runs instead of
the 30 he had compiled the year before, but he had 30 doubles
compared to 18 in 1959. He had played in 144 games in 1960
as against 150 in 1959 and had 126 hits as compared with 149
the year before. And American League pitchers had shown
him respect by pitching with great care to him all season long,
with the result that he had 92 bases on balls, third highest in
the league.

After the season Allison, always a thinking player, benefited
by hindsight in his analysis of his problems.

"I think it may have been mental as much as anything," he
decided. "I had the tendency for a while not to really think
about what I was doing. I guess I expected everything to be
the same as the year before, and I shouldn't have figured that

way. The pitchers in this league are too smart, for one thing. As a result, I found my hitting falling off and I couldn't seem to correct it. Anyway, I'm going to do my best to give the team a better year next season."

Bob Allison, who was never satisfied with anything less than perfection, was far from satisfied with his 1960 performance.

9

The day was October 26, 1960. In a large conference room in the Savoy-Hilton Hotel in New York, officials of the American League and the individual club owners sat around a highly polished table and voted to expand the league to ten teams.

As far as the baseball world in general was concerned, this was the big news that came out of the top-level meeting. But to Calvin Griffith and the Washington Senators, another decision made that day was of more personal interest. The clubs had granted permission to the Washington Senators to move their franchise to the twin cities of Minneapolis and St. Paul in Minnesota.

The maneuvering practiced that day, however, did not leave the nation's capital without a big league team. A new team was to be moved into Washington (the ninth in the expansion) and the tenth team would represent Los Angeles.

The news that Minneapolis–St. Paul would at last have a big league team was greeted with enthusiasm in that far north metropolis. It was a big day for the Chambers of Commerce in both Minneapolis and St. Paul, a bury-the-hatchet day, in fact. A spirited feud had been going on for some time between the two cities, about baseball as well as many other things. Located on opposite sides of the Mississippi River, they were natural rivals. Both had been advocating sites for the new ball park, should a big league team ever come to the area. Minneapolis people wanted it on their side; St. Paul was just as determined to have it on theirs. But at last the dispute was settled by mutual agreement: the new ball park would be located in Bloomington, south of the Twin Cities and about an equal distance from each.

Only the problem of a name for the team remained, and so that neither city would gain the upper hand in this respect, it was decided to call the team the Minnesota Twins, the first major league ball club to be named after a state instead of a city.

When Bob Allison heard of the move to the Twin Cities he was immediately enthusiastic.

"I understand there are a lot of good business opportunities for the off-season up there," he told Betty. "Maybe I ought to go up and investigate."

So Allison became the first player to actually migrate to the Twin Cities area. There he met Gerald L. Moore, executive vice-president of the Minneapolis Chamber of Commerce, and one of the prime leaders in the bond campaign to build the new Metropolitan Stadium in Bloomington. Moore introduced Bob to Tom Moore, Jr., an executive with the Coca-Cola Bottling Company. Allison was offered a public relations job during the non-baseball months and accepted the position immediately. Then he went back to Washington and in November moved his family to the Twin Cities.

During the winter of 1960–1961, Bob, his wife, and two boys found that the weather in Minnesota was somewhat different from that of Raytown, Missouri. But the Allisons quickly learned to love the winter. The family went ice skating for the first time in their lives, and Bob got in some experience in ice fishing and hunting.

Only one thing bothered Bob Allison—the memory of his unsettled stomach during the past baseball season. He wanted to make certain that there was nothing wrong with him physically, and during the early winter he visited the Mayo Clinic in Rochester, Minnesota, for a complete examination. The doctors found nothing organically wrong.

"Athletic stomach," was their decision. "Nothing alarming."

The diagnosis erased Bob's concern, and he not only enjoyed a pleasant season of winter sports and work with the Coca-Cola Bottling Company, but looked forward with a quiet determination to a new "start" with the Minnesota Twins.

There was a new spirit in the camp at Orlando, Florida, when the newly formed Minnesota Twins took the field. Everyone felt that the sad second-division days at Washington were over. They were now a brand-new team, representing a new city, and the future looked bigger and brighter for all of them. Although the Twins put together only a mediocre 14–14 record in the Grapefruit League in 1961, there was no mistaking the feeling of enthusiasm that was sweeping the camp. The experts were picking the Twins to finish anywhere from fourth to sixth, but Cookie Lavagetto was more optimistic.

"We're going to surprise a lot of people," he said to a sportswriter. "We've got all the makings of a good ball club."

Bob Allison, as was always the case, played every exhibition game as if the World Series was at stake. Calvin Griffith, sitting in the stands with a sports scribe one day, shook his head in dismay at Bob's hustle.

"I like the way he bears down," he said. "He's great now,

when he's pushing himself. If he ever learns to relax, he'll be one of the best players in the American League."

The new Minnesota Twins opened the season in 1961 against New York at Yankee Stadium, an extreme test for this new team with its new spirit. Before the start of the game sports-writers crowded around Lavagetto, anxious for a rundown on the Twins. Most of them were dubious about where the team would finish. All agreed that Minnesota had power to burn. But they were not sure that the Twins' pitching was up to major league standards, and they looked with some suspicion at the team's fielding. It seemed like the old Washington team all over again, in a new setting.

Actually, the lineup that took the field in the opener was impressive, at least on paper.

Leading off for the Twins was Zoilo Versalles, who looked as if he might become one of the league's outstanding short-stops. Following him in the batting order were Len Green, center field; Harmon Killebrew, first base; Jim Lemon, left field; Bob Allison, right field; Earl Battey, catching; Reno Bertoia, third base; Billy Gardner, second base; and Pedro Ramos, pitching.

Whitey Ford, the Yankee ace, was on the mound for the Bronx Bombers in the opener. His assortment of fast balls and slants could give the best hitters in the game nightmares, and when the game got under way he immediately began to exhibit his mastery. For six innings he held Minnesota scoreless, and it looked as if he might coast to victory if the Yankees could get him a few runs. The trouble was, they couldn't. Ramos was pitching just as good a game as Ford, and at the end of the sixth the score was deadlocked, 0–0.

It was windy in Yankee Stadium that day and high fly balls were doing tricks in the air. Allison, in right field, made several good catches of towering flies blown by the wind, and Lava-getto kept nodding his head pleasantly as he observed Bob's talents in the field. But no one was hitting, including Allison, until the seventh inning came along.

Bob Allison was leadoff man in the top of the seventh, and the crafty Ford went to work on him. The first pitch was a teaser just outside for a ball. The next one was a blazer that cut the plate for a strike. Bob fouled the third pitch off. Then Whitey tempted him with a change-up, but it was outside and Allison let it go by. Two and two.

Allison expected the fast ball next, and he got it. Bob swung. The ball shot on a line to left field and dropped into the stands 315 feet away.

The home run ignited a rally that saw the Twins score three times, and in the bottom half of the frame Ramos held the Yanks scoreless again.

In the eighth inning Allison again found himself at the plate with the bases empty. This time he measured Whitey Ford for a single to center. Although Earl Battey forced Allison at second, Reno Bertoia then contributed a home run to make the score 5–0 in favor of the Twins. They tallied one more in the ninth to make the final score 6–0.

Allison's two hits in five times up had started two rallies that won the game for the Twins. And Ramos let the vaunted Yanks down with three hits.

The Twins had posted a win in their opener, and Allison and Bertoia were the clubhouse heroes of the day.

The second game against the Yanks was rained out and the Twins moved on to Baltimore. Here they squeezed out a 3–2 win with Allison getting one-for-three and Camilo Pascual striking out twelve Oriole batsmen. But the next day the roof fell in. Not only did Baltimore whip the Twins 8–0, but Harmon Killebrew pulled a hamstring muscle in his leg and the doctors estimated he would be out of the lineup for three weeks, a sad blow to the resurgent Twins.

The next day the Twins played a doubleheader at Baltimore's

Memorial Stadium. In the first game, the Twins jumped on starting pitcher Chuck Estrada in the first inning. When Allison came up for his turn at bat he found the bases loaded with Minnesota runners.

Estrada decided that giving Allison a fast ball in this situation was suicide, so he tried to curve him to death. The first pitch was a sweeping curve that caught the outside edge of the plate for a called strike. Then he got one in too tight for a ball. The next offering was a change-up, and Allison was out in front of it, pulling it into the stands back of third.

With two strikes against him Allison was forced to protect the plate—and he did. He hit the next pitch far into the left-field stands for a grand-slam homer!

In the sixth inning Allison came up with two Twins on the sacks. Reliefer Dick Hall was now on the mound for the Orioles. Allison promptly drilled another home run into the left-field seats. The final score was Twins 10, Orioles 5, with Allison having batted in seven of the ten runs.

In the clubhouse between games sportswriters clustered around the big outfielder.

"Ever knock in seven runs in one game before?" someone asked.

"No, I don't think so," said Allison. "I don't ever remember doing it."

"How many grand-slam homers have you hit, Bob?"

"This is my second," said Allison.

"Do you remember your first?"

Allison grinned. "How could I forget that first one? It was during my first year in the majors, 1959, and it was our first trip to Chicago. I hit it off Early Wynn. I'll always remember that one."

"And two homers in one game—how often have you done that?"

"Twice, I think. Last year and the year before."

One of the sportswriters made a premature remark, then, to the effect that Bob Allison was already ahead of Babe Ruth's famous record of sixty homers in a season. Bob laughed it off.

"That may be so," he said, "but I'm not worried about catching Ruth. I just want to keep on hitting, and I'll take the homers as they come."

Across the room Pedro Ramos, the winning pitcher, was making a few comments of his own.

"I was staggering out there," he said. "But as long as I got that big Bob Allison on my side, I'm okay."

Having racked up four wins and one loss on their opening road trip, the Minnesota Twins flew to Minneapolis. On the evening of April 20, the combined Minneapolis–St. Paul Chambers of Commerce gave the team a "Meet the Twins" Banquet at the Hotel Raddison in downtown Minneapolis. City officials and other dignitaries greeted their new team with enthusiasm and made the Twins feel that they were an important part of the Twin Cities culture. Newspapers headlined the arrival of "the first major league ball team in the history of the Twin Cities."

The next day the Twins received their first look at their new ball park. Metropolitan Stadium—which later was to become known as the Met—was new, fresh-looking and inviting. The grass in the outfield was a close-clipped green carpet, and the infield was manicured to perfection. It had a seating capacity of 40,000 and to a team loaded with long-ball hitters it looked like paradise.

The left- and right-field foul line measurements were 330 feet. Center field was 412. But it was the distance in right center and left center that intrigued the power hitters. This area is known as "home run alley"—where most of the pull hitters, depending on whether they hit right-handed or left-handed, hit their longest drives. The distances here measured 350 feet, a healthy poke but not an insurmountable one.

"The park seems ready-made for home runs," said Allison
with a speculative gleam in his eye.

"Yes," said Killebrew. "I think you could hit some out of
here."

A capacity crowd showed up to see the new Minnesota
Twins in their debut. They were enthusiastic fans, noisy and
in a mood to celebrate. What bothered the Twins more than
anything else was that they let the home fans down in the
first game. A ragtag Washington outfit made up of leftover
players from other teams in the league beat the Twins,
5–3.

The next day, however, the Twins edged the same team,
5–4, in ten innings of exciting baseball.

A few days later the Twins were engaged in a critical game
with the Los Angeles Angels—critical because first place in
the league standings was at stake. Earl Battey was hot that
day, pacing the Minnesota hitters, and when the ninth inning
opened the Twins had a 4–2 lead.

But the Angels refused to roll over and play dead. They
rallied in the ninth inning, putting two men on base with two
out and bringing Ken Hunt to bat.

Allison knew that Hunt was capable of hitting a long ball,
and he backed up near the warning track in right field. The
tying runs were on the bases, and Hunt, if he could get one
out of the park, represented the winning run.

Camilo Pascual was the Twins' hurler, and he worked diligently on Hunt. But Hunt tagged one. He sent it towering into
right field and Allison raced back to the screen. For a moment
Bob thought the ball would go in with plenty to spare, but
then he saw that he had a chance, an outside chance, to catch
it.

Allison timed his leap with precision, going up with his
gloved hand stretched above his head. The ball slammed into
the webbing of his glove and stuck. The leaping grab robbed

Hunt of a winning homer and ended the game with a Twin victory.

In the clubhouse, Pascual threw his arms around Allison in a bear hug.

"Thanks for that catch," he said. "You're my buddy!"

The win gave the Minnesota Twins sole possession of first place with a 9–3 record. Right behind them were the Tigers with 8–2 and New York with 7–4.

Allison continued to play the game of baseball the only way he knew how—hard. The next day he hit a double in the sixth inning in a seesaw affair with the Angels and had to slide into second. He did it in his usual style, hitting the dirt late and going into the bag full tilt.

Ken Aspromonte leaped out of the way of Allison's slide and put the ball on him high and hard. It was too late and Aspromonte glared down at Allison.

"Someday," he said angrily, "you oughta learn how to slide."

Allison got up and brushed off his trousers.

"Sorry," he said, grinning, "but that's the only way I know how to do it."

Despite Allison's efforts, however, the Twins dropped the game to the Angels, 6–5, in twelve innings, and the loss dumped them into second place. The Detroit Tigers now had the top spot and the Yanks were third.

In early May, Bob Allison's hitting tailed off. Suddenly the ball wasn't falling in for him, and his batting average started to slide. Allison tried to fight his way out of it, even refusing to acknowledge that he was in a slump.

"I'm not in a slump," he told a writer. "I hit the ball hard but it's always at somebody."

Slump or no slump, Allison was a standout in the field. He made a number of dazzling catches and kept runners glued to the bases with bullet-like throws from the outfield. One of the key plays in a 2–0 victory by Camilo Pascual over the Kansas City Athletics was a strong throw from the right-field corner

that caught Dick Howser trying to stretch a single into a
double.

"That's one of the things I like about Bob," Lavagetto said.
"When he's in a hitting slump, he doesn't let it affect his
fielding. In fact, he seems to play harder in the field. That boy
can win you a lot of games defensively too."

But when Allison's slump persisted into mid-May, Lavagetto was forced to take action.

"I'm going to have to bench you," he said to Bob. "Maybe
a few days' rest will help straighten you out."

Allison had the normal ballplayer's dislike of sitting on the
bench, but he could see the wisdom of Lavagetto's decision.

"Maybe you're right, Cookie," he said. "I'm willing to try
anything to shake this hitting lag."

Allison squirmed impatiently on the bench for two days.
Then, on May 13, Lavagetto put him back in the lineup.

"This is the day to break out of it," the manager said.

As he and Killebrew walked through the tunnel to the dugout, Allison grinned half-sadly. "I hope he's right," he said.

The Twins were playing the Los Angeles Angels that day,
and Jerry Casale was the opposing pitcher. In his first turn at
bat Allison grounded out, but when he came to bat for the
second time, he rewrote the script. It was the third inning and
Earl Battey had singled and Jim Lemon had walked ahead of
him. The score was knotted at 3–3.

Casale threw Bob everything in the book, a sharp curve, a
slider, a fast ball. The next pitch was a slow-breaking curve,
away from the batter, and Allison caught it on the fat of the
bat. The ball soared like a rocket into the left-field stands for a
three-run homer, his sixth of the year.

The hit started the Twins on the road to victory, but before
the game was over Allison hit a second home run and a single
to go three-for-four.

"It looks like you've broken the slump," commented Killebrew, always happy to see his friend do well.

"I hope so," said Allison. "It was a mighty pleasant day."

Allison had batted in five runs and taken the club lead with a total of twenty-one. He was batting .250, with seven home runs. The Twins were in third place, trailing the New York Yankees in second and the Detroit Tigers in first.

Then came disaster.

10 ⚾

It developed that Bob Allison had broken his slump for only one day. His sudden resurgence did not last. Nor did the Twins profit during the month of May. They tumbled into a disastrous losing streak. The hitters failed, fielding was not up to par, and the pitching turned sour. By the end of May the Twins found themselves in seventh place.

Nobody worried more about the Twins' plight than Allison himself. He hated to lose ball games. He particularly hated to lose them in bunches. In attempting to analyze the games the team lost, he was in effect assuming all of the manager's worries. Random thoughts would race through his mind:

"Maybe we should have bunted in the eighth instead of hitting straightaway and into a double play."

"Maybe we shouldn't have taken our pitcher out so early."

"Maybe we shouldn't have left our pitcher in so long."

"If I had just been able to get a long fly with that man on third instead of a pop-up, we'd have had the tying run in."

Bob knew he was second-guessing, but he couldn't help it. He was vitally concerned with the collapse of the Twins.

So was President Calvin Griffith. As usual, when a team hits the doldrums, the front office begins to think of trades that might strengthen the club. All through May there were rumors that Griffith was willing to make a big trade at any time if he thought he could improve the team. Newspapers reported that there were only four players Griffith would not trade—Len Green, Harmon Killebrew, Zoilo Versalles and Earl Battey. He had reached a point of desperation, the newspapers said, that made him willing to trade Camilo Pascual, Pedro Ramos—or even Bob Allison!

"I like Bob personally," he said to a writer asking him about the big slugger. "But an owner can't have any favorites. I have to do what I think will strengthen the team. I'll say one thing, though. If we parted with Allison, it would have to be a big trade, a *really* big trade!"

Bob Allison spent a few sleepless hours thinking about Griffith's statement. It was gratifying to know that the Twins considered him so valuable that only a big trade of front-line players would trigger his departure. But, on the other hand, the mere fact that his name was dangled about as trade bait shook him severely.

The month of June started off with some maneuvering on the part of Calvin Griffith that startled the team. In the first two days of the month the Twins pulled two trades. On June 1 they peddled infielder Billy Consolo to the Milwaukee Braves and received second baseman Billy Martin, once a Yankee, in return. At the same time the Twins sent Paul Giel and Reno Bertoia to the Kansas City Athletics in exchange for outfielder Bill Tuttle.

On June 2 the Twins optioned infielder Don Mincher to Buffalo in the International League and picked up first baseman–outfielder Julio Becquer, who had been up before, to bolster the bench. The club also signed Bernie Allen, a Purdue University shortstop, to a $50,000 bonus, and got the name of Joe Nossek, of Ohio University, on a contract.

In all this juggling, the acquisition of outfielder Bill Tuttle seemed to pose the gravest threat to Allison. Tuttle was an experienced man and could well take Allison's place in the lineup if Bob's slump continued.

The threat appeared immediately menacing when Lavagetto approached Allison in the clubhouse before a doubleheader with the Detroit Tigers.

"I want to get Tuttle in the lineup," he said frankly. "I'd like to play you at first base, Bob."

Allison was startled. He had played only two games at first base in his life, but he was willing to make a try at it if that was what Lavagetto wanted.

"I'll play anywhere you think I can help the team," he said. "Good."

It was a desperation move on Lavagetto's part because the Twins had at this time lost twelve of their last thirteen games. All the shuffling of personnel didn't seem to help, either, because the Tigers whipped the Twins twice to extend their losing streak to fourteen out of the last fifteen. Then the Yanks came in, beat the Twins twice more, and the record became sixteen losses in seventeen games.

And the Twins were now in eighth place.

An uneasy tension swept the club. Trade talk and speculation grew. Top management wanted to have a winning team in their first year in Minnesota, and the word was out that Calvin Griffith was getting impatient. Maybe, the papers said, the trades had only begun. If things got much worse, there might be a wholesale trading-bee before long.

Then came a peculiar move that raised questions all over the league. At exactly 3:30 P.M. on June 6, Cookie Lavagetto was eased out. Sam Mele, former American League first baseman and outfielder, and a coach of the Twins, was designated as the man who would take over.

"So Lavagetto's fired?" asked a reporter.

"No, he's not fired," said Griffith. "He's been given a week's furlough. Mele is to run the club in his absence."

It was a curious situation, to say the least. Lavagetto was enjoying a vacation, no doubt imposed on him, and Mele was running the club as a sort of interim manager.

The first game played with Mele at the helm turned out to be an unusual one. The Yanks were in town, and in the third inning of the game, at exactly 8:30 P.M., the Twins' Ron Henry was called out on strikes. Mele protested to umpire Bill Stewart, and when he protested with too much vigor, he was thumbed out of the game. Ed Lopat, the Twins' pitching coach, then took over.

Thus in five hours—from 3:30 P.M. to 8:30 P.M.—the Twins had three "managers," Lavagetto, Mele and Lopat!

Even with three managers, however, the Twins couldn't win. The Yanks beat Minnesota again to extend their losses to seventeen out of the last eighteen games. The next day the Yankees repeated their win to make it eighteen out of nineteen!

Meantime, despite the depressing losing streak, Allison was taking over first base with surprising efficiency. He seemed to instinctively know how to make all the moves around the bag, and he was a big target for the infielders to throw at. But even more important, Allison's hitting began to pick up in June again. The slump was over.

The weird juggling of Twins' personnel was not over, however. On June 13 Lavagetto returned and took back the management of the club, and Mele returned to his coaching job. The Twins were now in ninth place. This arrangement lasted for ten days, and on June 23 the ax fell with a final thud. Lavagetto was fired and Sam Mele was officially made manager of the team.

Mele showed at once that he had different ideas about how to use Bob Allison to the best advantage. His first lineup had Julio Becquer on first base and Allison back in right field.

"It's where I really belong," Allison conceded.

The Twins won their first game under Mele, posting a 4–0

win over New York with Camilo Pascual hurling a dazzling six-hitter.

On June 27 the Twins met Boston in a memorable double-header at Minnesota's Metropolitan Stadium. The Twins edged Boston in the first game, 6–5, and sensed an opportunity to gain some of the ground they had lost if they could put the second game on the winning side of the ledger.

The score was 0–0 in the fourth when Gene Conley, the Boston pitcher, got himself into trouble. Green was first up for the Twins and Conley walked him. Conley worked too carefully on the dangerous Killebrew and also gave him a free pass to first. Jim Lemon, a slugger who ordinarily could be expected to hit straightaway, laid down a sacrifice bunt to move the runners up. Conley leaped on the ball like a cat and whipped it to first. But his throw was wide, pulling the first baseman off the bag, and all runners were safe.

Bases loaded and Bob Allison up.

Conley fidgeted on the mound. He picked up the resin bag, hitched up his trousers, adjusted his cap, and finally toed the rubber. He went into a short stretch, cast an apprehensive glance at the base runners, and threw the first pitch to Allison. Bob let it go by and the umpire went up with his right hand.

"Stee-rike!"

Allison stepped out of the batter's box and did a little fidgeting of his own. He knocked dirt out of his spikes, picked up dirt in his hand, wiped his hand on his trousers, then carefully took his wide stance in the box.

Conley delivered. It was a curve that hung. Allison straightened it out. The ball went screaming 380 feet over the screen in left center. The homer was his thirteenth of the year and represented his forty-eighth RBI. It propelled the Twins to a 6–3 victory.

And it was his second grand-slam homer of the season.

Allison hit another round-tripper before June was out, and

on July 3 the Chicago White Sox came to Met Stadium for a series. The first game was a tight one, and the score was 3–3 when the last of the seventh opened.

Turk Lown was on the hill for the Sox, and he easily retired the first two Minnesota batters in the seventh. But then he pitched too finely to Bill Tuttle and walked him. Pascual was up, and when he bounced to the usually reliable Nellie Fox at second, it looked as if Lown was safely out of the inning. But Fox bobbled the ball and there were two runners on the bags.

Billy Martin was up next and he topped a pitch along the third base line, beating it out for a scratch hit. The bases were loaded again as Allison strode to the plate.

Lown looked the big slugger over and toed the rubber. He was determined not to give Allison anything good to hit. But at the same time he had to be careful not to walk him and force in the go-ahead run.

The first pitch was a ball outside. The next was a curve that Allison fouled back against the screen. The third pitch was a fast ball, low. Obviously, Lown intended to keep the ball outside to Allison so he couldn't pull it, and low in the hope that he would hit it into the ground.

Lown got a second strike across to even the count at two-and-two. Allison swung his bat in arcs at the plate, ready now to swing at anything that looked near the strike zone. Lown came in with it, but the pitch was in the dirt.

Ball three, strike two.

The runners, eager, danced off the bags. With a full count and two out, they were poised to set sail with the pitch. Lown delivered and the runners broke. The ball came in belt-high and Allison swung. The sharp *crack* sounded good to Bob's ears. The ball rose in a high arc and landed 400 feet away in the left-center-field seats. It made the score 7–3 and the Twins finally won the game, 7–6.

The grand-slam homer was Allison's third of the year and the second in a week!

There was no longer any doubt that Allison's slump was over, but a new dimension had been added to the big out-fielder's hitting. Allison's teammates noticed an important fact about Bob's long-distance clouting—more and more he was getting his hits with men on base, with the score tied late in the game, in crucial situations.

"He's Mr. Clutch," said someone in the clubhouse, and the name stuck.

"He is a great clutch hitter," Mele admitted. "I like to see him up there in a crucial spot. That's when he seems to deliver the best."

The nickname, Mr. Clutch, wasn't exactly popular with Bob Allison. He had his usual analytical answer to his clutch hitting.

"A pitcher is more apt to make a mistake in the clutch and give you a good ball to hit," he said. "With no one on, a pitcher can relax. Anyway, I'm unhappy about the number of times I strike out. I've got to do something about that."

Allison was again showing his desire for nothing less than perfection, but he had been tagged Mr. Clutch and there wasn't much he could do about it. At the All-Star Game break on July 11 he was leading the Twins with sixty RBI's on sixty-seven hits, and Mele rewarded him for this performance by giving him the clean-up spot in the batting order.

"That's where he belongs," Mele said, "where he can drive in our guys."

"I guess the RBIs and homers mean the most in the long run," Bob admitted, "but I sure would like to cut down my strikeouts. And I could stand a better batting average too." He was hitting .229.

League competition took time out while the American and National League players went at each other in the All-Star Game at windswept Candlestick Park in San Francisco. Despite all his heroics, Allison did not appear in the All-Star contest; Killebrew and Pascual were the only two Twins chosen. The National League edged the American League, 5–4.

The Twins resumed the regular schedule in an unenviable position following the All-Star classic. They were still in eighth place, eighteen and a half games behind the league-leading Detroit Tigers.

In mid-July, Allison became involved in one of the most unusual double plays in baseball history. The Twins were meeting the Indians at Cleveland, and Dick Stigman was on the hill for the Tribe. In the fourth inning Killebrew opened with a single. Julio Becquer flied out and Allison walked. Runners were now on first and second with one out.

Hal Naragon hit the first pitch and drove a ground ball toward second baseman Johnny Temple. Allison headed for second base but he had no chance. Temple tossed the ball to shortstop Mike de la Hoz for an easy force-out. In fact, Allison was only about three fourths of the way to the bag when the force play was made.

That was his undoing. The Indian shortstop whipped the ball toward first to complete the twin killing. Allison, racing into second, saw a white blur in front of him, and then the ball hit him in the head. Allison dropped in his tracks.

The ball bounced off his head as Killebrew rounded third and headed home. As luck would have it, the ball bounded toward home plate. Catcher John Romano scooped it up and tried to tag Killebrew, but he was too late. Romano then threw to first baseman Tito Francona to double Naragon who had made a wide turn at first and couldn't get back!

Allison, feeling whoozy, was rushed to a Cleveland hospital for x-rays, but there was no fracture.

"I guess you might say that I had a run butted in," he said with a grin.

Whether he butted them in or batted them in, Allison's remarkable clutch hitting continued through the 1961 season. A case in point was July 28 when the Twins met the Tigers at Tiger Stadium in Detroit. Allison came up in the first inning with Len Green, who had walked, on base. Paul Foytack was pitching for the Tigers, and he was a pitcher who could be very tough if he was right. But Allison solved his delivery. He drove a home run into the left-field stands to give the Twins a 2–0 lead.

The lead held up until the sixth, when the Tigers scored two to even the count. The teams struggled into the ninth inning, still deadlocked at two runs apiece.

The first two Twins went out easily in the ninth, but Killebrew reached first when shortstop Dick McAuliffe bobbled his grounder. Allison came up to face Foytack again. The Tiger pitcher was wary. The memory of Allison's first-inning homer was still fresh in his mind. Cagily, Foytack fed Bob three pitches—a strike on the corner and two near-misses. Then he curved him and Allison fouled it off.

A raucous-voiced fan let out a bellow: "Strike him out, Paul! Give him the dipsy-doo!"

Foytack didn't heed the fan's advice. He gave Allison a fast ball instead. It came in higher than he wanted and Bob swung. The ball rocketed into the left-field stands for Allison's second homer of the night, making the score 4–2. The Tigers scored once in the last of the ninth, but the Twins won the game, 4–3, with Allison having clutch-hit all the runs in.

The season wore on into August, and Allison happily continued to give nightmares to American League pitchers. Then, he received news from home that gave him even more incentive to continue his rampage. His wife had presented him with another son. The couple named the child Kyle Brent.

Allison ended the 1961 season with no letup in his bombardment, and the final statistics proved that he had experienced one of his finest seasons. Although he batted only .245, his ability to hit in the clutch had given him 105 runs batted in— the first time in either his major or minor league careers that he had passed the 100 mark in RBI's. In his collection of hits were 29 homers, only one less than his banner year of 1959, giving him seventh place in the league in both home runs and RBI's. He also posted his best fielding average, with .978, and his slingshot arm threw out 14 men on the bases during the 1961 season.

Mele had a parting comment about Allison's hitting as the season ended. "Don't let that batting average fool you," he said. "It's very misleading. He's one of the greatest clutch hitters in the game."

But despite Allison's performance and some outstanding seasons by several other Twins players, the Minnesota team finished seventh in their first season at the Twin Cities.

11

The growing family of Bob Allison and his wife had by now dictated a move to a larger home, and shortly before the end of the 1961 season the Allisons had settled in an attractive house in Edina, a suburb of Minneapolis not far from Metropolitan Stadium. About this same time a reporter interviewed Betty Allison to obtain her reaction to being the wife of a major league ballplayer. Her eyes sparkled at the question.

"Well, it's had both its problems and its fun," she said. "Up to now, we've never owned any furniture other than a TV set. Now that we're buying a house, we'll be starting from the beginning except for some wedding gifts we have stored at my parents' home, and which I haven't seen for five years. There's crystal and china and a lot of other things that will give us a start. But to answer your question, I've loved every minute of it. I love baseball and going to spring training every year."

Bob Allison kept busy during the winter with his Coca-Cola job. He moved out of public relations and proved to be an excellent salesman, calling on retail stores and restaurants to

sell pre-mix Coke and Bubble-Up. He would walk into a res-
taurant and say to the proprietor, "Hi, I'm Bob Allison."

Usually the proprietor would look at him a little doubtfully.

"Bob Allison, the ballplayer, you mean?"

"Sure," Bob would answer. "I work during the off-season for
the Coca-Cola Company."

That would break the ice, and after a handshake Bob would
say, "Aren't you getting tired of wrestling bottles around?"

"Well, yeah—I am tired of wrestling with them," the proprietor would say.

Allison then would proceed to sell him the pre-mix Coke and
Bubble-Up which came in a large steel bottle and was released
through a dispensing system.

By now Bob also had a television program going for him.
It was a local thirty-minute show consisting of taped inter-
views with sport personalities. Bob also answered questions
sent in by fans.

In addition to all this, Allison's natural leadership qualities
had been recognized by his teammates, who had voted him
the official player representative for the Twins' ball club. To
this important job—in which he had to air player gripes with
top management—he brought a level-headedness that consistently paid off. One of his major accomplishments in this field
was arranging a schedule of personal appearances by ballplayers. The system was chaotic at the time, and Allison revised
it. Players would henceforth make one free appearance for
the club. After that they would be paid.

When he wasn't involved in some kind of work, Bob enjoyed the company of his family in winter sports in the Minneapolis area. And with a new baby in the family, he learned all
over again the art of changing diapers and feeding the infant.

Being close at hand was an advantage when it came to signing each year's baseball contract. Usually he got together personally with Calvin Griffith and ironed out the details. Allison
was by now becoming a well-paid major league star.

When Bob reported to Orlando for spring training in 1962, he arrived with perhaps more confidence than he had ever before enjoyed. After his big 1959 season he had hit the doldrums in 1960, a victim of what is sometimes called the sophomore jinx. But he had rebounded strongly in 1961 and was now, without a doubt, an established major league ballplayer of considerable importance to his team.

The Twins enjoyed a good spring training in 1962. Twin Cities' sportswriters lauded the team in their papers. One writer, seeking an evaluation of the team from a players' viewpoint, chose Allison because of his analytical mind.

"Where do you think the Twins will finish this year?" he asked.

Allison supplied his usual thoughtful answer. "I think we have the best all-around club I've seen since I came up," he said. "We have better defense, more pitching depth, and eight guys in the lineup that can hit the ball. We also have a winning complex. The guys believe in themselves, and a lot of the credit for this belongs to Sam Mele. I'd say we could finish in the first division this year."

The experts who judge the teams before the start of league play were in general agreement. Most of them picked the Twins for the first division.

But Calvin Griffith, never known for stand-pattism, was still attempting to strengthen the team. He wanted to get more defensive strength in the infield, and just before the season started he made a trade with the Cleveland Indians. He parted with one of his fine pitchers, Pedro Ramos, to get Vic Power for first base. Pitcher Dick Stigman also came to the Twins in the deal.

The trade firmed up the Twins' infield. Power was not only a good hitter but one of the finest defensive first basemen in the league. Rookie Bernie Allen was slated for second base, having been so impressive that he took the job away from veteran Billy Martin. Zoilo Versalles, a much improved player, was at short, and Rich Rollins was assigned the third base bag. In the outfield it would be Allison in right, Killebrew in left, and Green in center. This, with Jack Kralick selected to pitch the first game of the season, was the Twins' opening lineup.

Although the Twins got off on the wrong foot by losing the opener to Kansas City by a 4–2 score, they rebounded the next day with a lopsided 8–0 win. In this one Camilo Pascual pitched a four-hitter, and home runs by Bob Allison, Earl Battey and Rich Rollins highlighted the carnage.

A few days later the Twins met the Los Angeles Angels in a dingdong battle that reached the end of the ninth inning with the teams tied, 7–7. In the Twins' half of the tenth, Allison found himself at the plate with two Minnesota runners dancing eagerly on the bases. He promptly hammered a double against the screen in left center to bring both runners home. The game ended 9–7.

"I'm happy to see Mr. Clutch is at it again in 1962," said a player in the clubhouse.

The Twins moved slowly into contention in the first weeks of the 1962 season. They were in sixth place with a 9–9 record at the end of April, but by May 5 had climbed to fourth with a 12–10 won-lost record. Allison was hitting a neat .286 and had two more home runs to his credit.

By the middle of May the Twins had pushed their way into third place by winning nine out of twelve games. The Cleveland Indians were hanging on to the top spot, with the New York Yanks and Minnesota Twins trailing by a scant half-game.

So far the Twins were making the experts look like experts. They were high in the first division, and several important factors were keeping them up there. The team was known to have hitters, and they were producing as expected, but the fielding of the Power-Allen-Versalles-Rollins infield was better than anyone had imagined. The four starters on the pitching staff—Camilo Pascual, Jim Kaat, Jack Kralick and Dick Stigman—were all generally effective. And in addition, a bullpen of Lee Stange, Frank Sullivan and Ray Moore was on hand to quench any fires that might start.

On May 20 the Twins and Yankees met in a doubleheader that the sports scribes were already describing as crucial. The two teams were in a virtual tie for second place, only a few percentage points behind the league-leading Cleveland Indians. A double loss for either team would be, at least momentarily, disastrous.

The first game was a tense struggle that the Yankees finally won by a 4–3 score. This put the Twins squarely on the spot.

"This nightcap we've got to take," Mele said in the clubhouse between games. "We've got to get even with them again."

The second contest was every bit as tense as the first. When the regulation nine innings were completed, the two teams were tied at two-all. The tenth went by with no score, then the eleventh, and the twelfth.

Bob Allison was the lead-off man in the thirteenth. Jim Coates was on the mound for the New Yorkers. Coates' first two pitches were outside; then he came in with one. Allison clouted it far into the left-field corner and raced into second with a stand-up double.

Bernie Allen was the next hitter. He swung at the first pitch and dribbled a roller toward short. Allison, seeing that the shortstop would have little chance for a play anywhere, legged it to third. Allen beat out the scratch hit.

Runners on first and third and no one out.

Zoilo Versalles was up. He rapped a clothesline single into right field, and Allison scampered home with the go-ahead run.

A bunt single and an infield out got Allen across with the second run of the inning, and the Twins had a 4–2 lead in the thirteenth.

The lead held up and the Twins earned a vital split in the two games.

All during April and May, Allison was experiencing an unusual hitting season. Near the end of May he was batting .302 and getting his share of clutch hits. But home runs were not on the menu. He had only two, both hit in the first ten days of the season. Since that time, although he had garnered his share of hits, he had failed to hit one out of the park.

"I know that home runs aren't the answer to everything," Allison said to Killebrew once, "but I feel as if I should be getting more of them."

"Don't worry about homers," advised Harmon. "They'll come. Just stand up there and swing."

"You think I might be doing something wrong up there?" asked Allison seriously.

Killebrew laughed. "With a batting average of .302, I'd say you're doing a few things *right*," he replied.

When the home runs finally came they came in a rash. It was June 9 and the Twins were entertaining the Chicago White Sox at Met Stadium. Entertaining, however, is hardly the word, because the White Sox did the Twins in 8–5. However, Allison collected a home run off crafty Early Wynn—the first since the second week of the season and only the third of the campaign.

The next day the Twins defeated the White Sox, 11–7, and Allison contributed another homer to the cause. The win was important because it put Minnesota in first place. The New York Yankees and Cleveland Indians were now both one-half game behind.

Two days later the Twins traveled to Los Angeles to meet the Angels. It was a tight game with the Angels clinging to a precarious 2–1 lead when the top of the eighth came around. Ryne Duren was on the hill for the Angels, and he was completely befuddling the Twins with his blazing fast ball.

Duren opened the eighth by walking Rich Rollins. But he didn't permit the free ticket to first base to shake his confidence. While Rollins dawdled around the first base bag, Duren bore down and struck out both Killebrew and Don Mincher.

Bob Allison walked slowly to the plate, wondering what one had to do to get a hit off Duren. He made threatening motions with his bat, cocked it over his right shoulder and waited for the blur of Duren's fast ball. Duren complied. He hurled one right over the heart of the plate in a manner that said plainly, "I'm not afraid of you, Buster."

Allison stood with the bat on his shoulder as a curve folded over for a second strike. The chips were down now. Behind the pitcher, he had to swing at anything good. Duren, on the other hand, could afford to tease Allison with bad pitches.

Allison looked them over carefully and let two pitches go by for balls. With the count two-and-two, Duren went for his favorite pitch, the fast ball. Allison was expecting it. He swung and the ball landed 390 feet away in the left-field bullpen, giving the Twins a 3–2 lead. They won the game, 4–2.

It was only his fifth home run of the season, but Allison had smashed three of the five in the last three games.

"It looks like you're finding the range again," commented Killebrew after the game.

"It's about time," said Allison.

Although the home runs were now beginning to come, Allison continued to get other key hits. In a mid-June game against the Kansas City Athletics at Kansas City, Allison got the Twins off and running in the first inning. Ed Rakow was on the mound for the A's, and he opened the inning by walking Len Green. Vic Power popped up, but Rich Rollins hammered a single to right. Rollins then stole second, and there were runners on second and third with Allison at bat.

Allison looked over a couple of pitches, fouled one into the stands, and then lashed a single to right. Two runs raced across the plate.

Later Bob drove in another with a single and the Twins won the game, 9–4.

The following day the Twins won by the same score from Chicago, with four home runs leading the way—by Allison, Killebrew, Power and Kaat.

The Twins were now playing good ball, but the trouble was that New York, Cleveland and Los Angeles were also riding high. By the first of July the Minnesota Twins were in fourth place with forty-two wins and thirty-six losses. Cleveland was leading the parade, with New York and Los Angeles a half game behind and the Twins a game and a half off the pace. Allison's lofty batting average had fallen to .260, but he had thirty-one runs batted in and six homers.

During the early part of July, however, the Twins fell into a worrisome batting slump. Allison was still hitting with some consistency, and so was Killebrew, but the rest of the team was struggling. It was at times like this that Allison's natural leadership qualities took over. He seemed to excel both in the field and at bat when the going was toughest. This fact was not lost on either Mele or Griffith.

"Bob has his slumps and bad games like anyone else," Mele said, "but when things are really dragging, that's when he comes through for you. He's a good man to have up there in the clutch or when your whole team is slumping."

"He was a natural leader when he was in high school," remarked Griffith, "and he's shown the same quality up here."

An example of Allison's inspired play occurred in a game with the Boston Red Sox at Fenway Park on July 3. Boston took an early 2–0 lead, and Boston hurler Bill Monbouquette seemed firmly in control of the situation. But Killebrew opened the third inning with a sharp single, and Rollins hit another that sent Killebrew thundering into third. It brought up Allison. He drove a Monbouquette slant over the inviting left-field wall, and the Twins had a lead that was never overcome. They won the game, 8–4.

Bob Allison again in 1962 found himself overlooked for the All-Star squad, but had he been selected to the American League team his clutch hitting might have come in handy. The National Leaguers beat the American League team, 3–1, in one of the All-Star Games' better pitching battles.

On July 18 the Twins emerged from their hitting slump with a bang that was heard all over the baseball world. The game was a record-setting contest involving the Twins and the Cleveland Indians at Minnesota.

Dick Stigman took the hill for the Twins and held the Indians scoreless in the top half of the first. Cleveland's Barry Latman started for the Indians—and the Twins immediately greeted him like a long-lost cousin.

Before Latman knew what stadium he was playing in, the Twins loaded the bases, bringing up the dangerous Allison. Latman looked around in some puzzlement at the number of men suddenly on the bases and delivered a cautious pitch. That was it. Allison promptly drilled it into the left-field seats for his eleventh home run of the season and fifth grand-slam homer of his career.

But that was only the beginning. Latman took an early shower, and Jim Perry came in to take up Cleveland's pitching burden. Before he had hardly warmed up, the Twins had loaded the bases again. This time Killebrew hammered one into the stands for another grand-slam homer. It was the first time in major league history that two batters had hit grand-slam homers in one inning!

He had hardly warmed up when the Twins had loaded the fourteen batters taking part in the slaughter. They went on to win an easy game, 14–3.

After the game, flashbulbs popped all over the clubhouse, as Allison and Killebrew posed for pictures.

"You guys know you set a record with those two grand-slam homers in the first inning, don't you?" a sportswriter asked.

"That's what we've been told," said Allison.

"What do you think about it?"

"Well, it's just one of those things," Allison said. "I don't think either Harmon or I was consciously swinging for the fences. We were just trying to hit the ball safely and both drives went out."

Killebrew agreed. "That's right. Home runs are the end result of a good swing at the ball. If you try for home runs you find you don't get them. If you just try to meet the ball, that's when they come.

"Do you think this ought to snap the team out of its hitting slump?" a reporter asked Mele.

"It ought to," said the manager, grinning. "We ought to bang the ball around a little from now on."

All through July the Twins were in relentless pursuit of first place. Most of the time they were a game or two behind, and as their hitting picked up again there was some cautious speculation that this might just be the year in which they would catch the Yanks.

Allison added fuel to the pennant fever the day after the record-breaking game with the Indians. He hit a bases-empty home run in the second inning, drove in another run with a single in the fourth, and hit a two-run homer in the eighth to lead the Twins to an 8–0 win over the Indians.

Later in the month, when the Twins were playing the Indians in Cleveland, Allison was again instrumental in posting a Twin victory. This game was a pitchers' battle with the Twins' Camilo Pascual opposing the Indians' Jim Perry. The Twins squeezed out a run in the first inning, and the Indians tied the score at 1–1 in the fourth. For eight innings that was all the scoring on either side.

In the top of the ninth, Perry continued his mastery over the Twins' batters. Vic Power raised a harmless fly behind second base for the first out, and Killebrew grounded to third for the second. Allison walked to the plate, wondering if the 1–1 tie would ever be broken.

Perry went into his windup and delivered the pitch. Bob looked at it but didn't offer.

"Stee-rike!" snarled the umpire.

It had been a fast ball and Allison figured a curve would be next. But Perry fooled him with another blazer, and Allison was caught looking.

"Stee-rike!" said the umpire again.

Allison stepped out of the box to collect his composure. Then he moved back in, dug a hole with his right toe, waved the bat at Perry threateningly.

Perry teased him with a pitch just outside. Then he came in tight on the handle. Allison swung at neither of them and the count was two-and-two.

A frog-voiced Cleveland fan was hollering to Perry to "strike 'im out!" Allison grinned. He knew that Perry would be more than happy to comply, if he could.

Perry came in with his hopping fast ball, and Allison brought the bat around. He caught the ball squarely and it rose on a slant and headed for the far confines of Cleveland's Municipal Stadium. It dropped with a clatter into the seats, and when Pascual set the Indians down without a score in the last half of the ninth, the Twins walked off with a dramatic 2–1 victory.

Mr. Clutch had come through again.

12

The fortunes of the Minnesota Twins skidded a little in the early days of August. Following the second All-Star Game on July 30—which the American League won, 9–4—the team began to lose a little ground to New York and Los Angeles in the pennant race. At the end of the first week of August, they found themselves five games behind the leading Yankees.

One day Calvin Griffith, watching Allison in the batting cage, called him over.

"You almost always pull the ball into left," he said, "and both infield and outfield play you as a pull hitter. You could improve your hitting a great deal if you drove the ball to all fields."

"I know you're right," Allison admitted, "but I just don't seem to be able to do it."

"Well," said Griffith, "there's a way you might accomplish it. Why don't you try a bigger and heavier bat? That will slow down your swing and should force you to hit to right and right-center more."

Allison recalled that Roy Sievers had advised the same thing back in 1959. Since that time, though, he had reverted to a thirty-three-ounce bat. Allison went promptly to the bat rack and selected one of Vic Power's thirty-six-ounce bats to replace his lighter warclub. The experiment worked. In the next few days Allison delivered a right-field home run and a right-center-field triple to confound opposing teams.

By mid-August the Twins were in danger of fading right out of the pennant race. They were now six and a half games behind the pace-setting Yankees, and the team was in another hitting slump. The Twins' fans, their hopes slipping, began to get impatient. There were some boos now when the Twins took the field.

"I hope they stick with us," said Allison. "We're trying to shake ourselves out of this. If we can do well against New York in our next series, we'll be right up there again."

The crucial series with New York started on August 14. At that time the Twins were an even six games behind the Yankees. The two teams were to meet in four games, and if either team could take three out of four it would provide a great impetus to go on to the pennant.

As it turned out, the series was inconclusive. The Twins won the first game, 6–4, the Yanks won the second and third games by 5–2 and 9–3 scores, and the Twins won the fourth contest, 9–8. An even split had done little to help either team.

Despite all these ups and downs, Bob Allison was making a strong contribution to the Twins' cause. He was now hitting .267, which was twenty-nine points higher than at the same time the year before, even though he had missed a number of games with minor injuries. With the heavier bat he was hitting more effectively to all fields, but he noticed one disadvantage to it, too. He was striking out more.

"Maybe it balances out," he said to Killebrew one day. "I gain something and I lose something."

But while Allison continued to hit, the rest of the team continued to slump. No one knows what causes a team to fall into a batting slump, and if anyone had a proven method for overcoming a slump, he could name his own price on any team in America. Usually a team emerges from a slump just as rapidly as it falls into one, and this is what happened to the Twins. Toward the last of August they began to hit again, and in the last few days of the month they managed to claw their way into second place, only two games behind the front-running Yankees.

"We aren't out of it yet," said Mele, and the Minneapolis–St. Paul newspapers picked up the refrain by reporting that the Twins might yet cop the pennant.

On August 29 the Twins were in Chicago for a go at the White Sox. The Sox, who could hardly be considered a pennant threat, were still in a position to spoil another team's chances, and they threw the skillful Ray Herbert at the eager Twins.

In the first inning Herbert got the first two Twins on easy outfield flies. But both Rich Rollins and Harmon Killebrew hit singles to bring up Allison. The big slugger from Raytown lost no time. He clobbered the first pitch 360 feet into the left-field seats to give the Twins three quick runs. It was his twentieth round-tripper of the season.

Before the inning was over, a double by Allen and a single by Versalles scored another run, and the count was 4–0.

The White Sox fought back, scoring three runs and crawling within one of a tie. But in the eighth the Twins added an insurance run when Rollins doubled, Killebrew scratched a single that moved Rollins to third, and Allison hit a high hopper to the infield that brought Rollins home. The final score was Twins 5, White Sox 3, Allison having driven in four of the five runs.

Early in September the Twins, still hot on the tail of the Yankees, moved to Washington to meet the Senators in a doubleheader. In the first game Allison homered off Marty Kutyna with Killebrew on base, a blow that helped the Twins post a 9–3 win. In the second game an unusual thing happened.

Washington was leading the Twins in the eighth inning, 3–1, and the Senators' pitcher, Ben Daniels, had the Twins swinging wildly at his assortment of slants.

In the eighth Vic Power led off with a single and Killebrew walked. Allison came up with a chance to drive in the tying runs.

Daniels didn't seem much impressed. He whipped over two fast strikes with a disdain that was obvious in the last row of the bleachers. Then, ahead of the batter, he teased Allison with a ball outside, making the count one-and-two.

Bob Allison knew that Daniels had a screaming fast ball working for him that day, and he felt that the pitcher would now go to this pitch for the strikeout. But Daniels fooled him—or almost did. He threw a curve, belt high and breaking away.

Expecting the fast one, Allison had gone too far with his swing to check it. Instead, when he saw the ball breaking away, he reached out and hit it—*one-handed*. The ball landed in the left-field bullpen 360 feet away! The one-handed homer put the Twins out front, 4–3, and that's the way the game ended.

In the clubhouse there was considerable discussion about the unusual home run.

"I was fooled," admitted Allison, "but I just reached out and got it with Vic Power's big bat."

A sportswriter went away shaking his head. "That guy Allison has enough power to knock 'em outa the park with one hand. Can you imagine that?"

"You write that in your story and none of your readers will believe it," said another.

In early September, Allison's hitting continued to spark the Twins. In Detroit he had another two-homer game when he hit his twenty-fourth with two on and another with the bases empty, both off Don Mossi.

But the New York Yankees continued to win, and the Twins were having a difficult time closing the gap. Finally, about mid-

September, the Twins began to fall behind. Within a week they found themselves five and a half games back of New York. On September 25 the Yankees officially clinched the American League pennant, and the Twins finished second, six games off the pace.

Although the Minnesota Twins failed to win the pennant in 1962, there was still reason for rejoicing in the club's front office. The team had skyrocketed from seventh place in 1961 to second in 1962, and attendance at Metropolitan Stadium had been good. And for 1963 the prospects looked excellent for an outstanding season—and maybe, this time, the winning of a pennant.

Bob Allison, spending his winter in his home at Edina, reflected on his contribution to the Twins' big year. It had been considerable. Driving in more than 100 runs for the second season in a row was an achievement of which he was proud, and with it he had kept up his pace of twenty-nine home runs. Baseball, always in Allison's blood, was boiling there now. He could hardly wait for spring training to come around as he looked forward to another big year with the club and the chance that they might go on to the pennant.

But spring training, 1963, turned out to be a fiasco for the team—and for Allison. The Twins simply could not get going during the Grapefruit League schedule. No one was hitting. Allison, Killebrew and Power—the big guns—were silent. The team seemed listless. They lost game after game, and some of the baseball analysts who had picked the Twins as a pennant threat were tempted to revise their estimates.

Calvin Griffith was never happy when the team was losing. One day during the Florida games when the Twins were staggering badly, he said to a writer, "I picked the Twins to win the pennant this year, and now we can't even win an exhibition game. But I still think we have a sound ball club. What we've got to do is put our hitting, pitching and fielding together, and I'm sure we'll do just that."

But the Twins didn't do just that—at least not in the exhibition games—and they eventually arrived in Minneapolis–St. Paul for their opener against the Cleveland Indians with a sad 7–20 record. Bob Allison, always concerned when the team did badly, nevertheless was confident the team would emerge from its slump in time to do mayhem in the American League race.

"That seven-twenty record won't affect the morale of this club once the season starts," he said. "The tempo is a lot different when league play begins. Players don't give as much in spring training. You think you're doing your best, but with nothing at stake, this isn't true. We'll get going as soon as the season starts."

Despite the poor preseason record, there were eight thousand fans on hand to greet the Twins when they landed at the Minneapolis airport. It was a welcoming that pleased all team members.

"I guess they haven't given up on us," said Allison gratefully.

"You have to go out and win for people like this," was Killebrew's comment.

"We'll shake up the league a little," Mele promised.

The Twins were invited to a "Meet the Twins" luncheon at the Pick-Nicollet Hotel in Minneapolis on the Monday preceding the opener, and the next day they clashed with the Cleveland Indians at Metropolitan Stadium. They presented substantially the same lineup that had taken second place the previous year— Len Green in center, Vic Power at first, Harmon Killebrew in left, Bob Allison in right, Bernie Allen at second, Earl Battey catching, George Banks replacing an injured Rich Rollins at third, Zoilo Versalles at shortstop and Camilo Pascual on the mound for the opener. Other top pitchers on the staff were Jim Kaat, Dick Stigman and Ray Moore.

But the problems that had plagued the Twins during spring

training pursued them into the regular season. The team lost four of its first five games, including the opener, and found themselves in last place at the end of the first week of play. In addition, Harmon Killebrew was in and out of the lineup with a sore knee, and his absence from the game did the team no good. Still, no one was panicking.

"I'm not down and the club isn't down," said Mele. "We'll bounce back. You can figure on it."

On April 16 Bob Allison took personal charge of the Twins' promised bounce-back. With Killebrew on the bench and rookie Jim Hall in center, the burden of carrying the club's hitting seemed to fall almost entirely on Bob's shoulders. He showed his leadership abilities again with a response that was electric.

The Los Angeles Angels were in Bloomington for a game, and the contest turned out to be a free-swinging slugging match. The Angels scored a run in the first, and the Twins came back with two in their half of the frame. Los Angeles went ahead, 4–2, in the third, and the Twins scored once to make it 4–3. The Angels made it 5–3 in the fourth, and in the bottom half of the fifth the Twins fought back to tie the score, 5–5.

But again the Angels went ahead by scoring two in the top of the seventh to make the score 7–5. This was the way the score stood as the Twins came up for their last chance in the bottom of the ninth.

The ninth didn't begin well at all, and the Twins found themselves on the brink of defeat. Len Green opened the inning with an easy fly to center, and Vic Power popped to first. Rookie Jim Hall, battling for a place on the team, doubled. It was Bob Allison's turn to bat.

He didn't wait. He picked out the first pitch and drove a clutch two-run homer into the left-field seats that deadlocked the score at 7–7.

Neither team scored in the tenth, but in the top of the eleventh the Angels posted two more runs on the scoreboard and again the Twins teetered on the edge of defeat. But, amazingly, they blasted their way back with two runs in their half of the inning to tie the score again, 9–9.

The twelfth inning was scoreless for both sides, and in the top of the thirteenth the Angels pushed across another run. Once more the Twins would have to come from behind to tie the score or win the game.

Vic Power opened the bottom half of the thirteenth with a sharp single to left. Hall bounced to short and forced Power at second.

Allison lifted a long fly to left, and the ball skidded off Leon Wagner's glove for an error. Allison was safe at first and Hall reached second. Bernie Allen ripped a single to center, and Hall scored the run that again tied the game, 10–10. On the same hit Allison raced to third.

When Mele sent Bill Tuttle up to pinch-hit, the Angels countered by walking him intentionally, loading the bases and setting up a play at any base. The only man they were worried about was Allison on third, since he represented the winning run.

But the strategy backfired when Eli Grba walked George Banks to force Bob in with the winning run in a tense, dramatic 11–10 victory.

After the game Mele commented that the slugging match had been Allison's greatest all-around game, and Bob agreed. He had been an instrument in most of the runs scored. In the first inning he had singled to drive in a run. In the third he drove in another with a long sacrifice fly. In the fifth he singled home still another. In the seventh he walked to prolong a rally. In the ninth he hit his clutch two-out two-run homer to knot the score at 7–7. In the eleventh he beat out an important infield hit that enabled the Twins to tie the score again, 9–9. In the thirteenth he reached first on Wagner's outfield error and lived to score the winning run when Grba forced him in with a bases-loaded walk.

Allison had gone four-for-five, and Mele commented that his 425-foot homer in the ninth inning was the "clutch hit of the year."

But Allison was pleased with the dramatic victory from another standpoint. "This kind of a win was just what we needed," he said in the clubhouse. "We were fighting from behind all day long. I've never seen our club fight back like we did today. It's the kind of shot in the arm you need when things are not going right."

For Allison, however, they were going very right indeed. He was off to the best start of his career, hitting .435 with ten hits in twenty-three trips.

Unfortunately, the dramatic come-from-behind victory over the Angels did not immediately snap the Twins out of the doldrums—and as a result Allison received one of his severest tests. It is a mark of a good ballplayer when he is able to continue playing in an outstanding manner while the rest of the team sags, and Allison met this challenge in the early days of the 1963 season. He not only continued his heavy hitting but made some remarkable catches in the outfield and came up with a few "impossible" throws. Mele was the first to notice it.

"He's a natural leader," the manager said again. "With Killebrew out, Allison has really taken charge. He has never been better in the field or at bat. He's doing his best to snap the team out of it."

And snapping the Minnesota Twins out of it was a man-sized job. By the end of April the team had won eight, lost ten and were bogged down in seventh place. It was hardly an inspiring spot for a team that had finished second the year before and were tabbed as a pennant winner in 1963.

In early May the Twins tumbled into last place, and the groans could be heard all over Minneapolis–St. Paul. Allison was leading the team in batting average, home runs and RBI's, but the team as a whole was dragging its heels. By May 15 they had won eleven, lost nineteen, and Calvin Griffith was making hopeful statements like, "Don't worry—we'll be up there at the finish."

These days were tense and worrisome ones for Bob Allison. It was his nature to worry about the team, almost in the same manner the manager worried, and he tried hard to spark the team both by his own play on the diamond and by inspirational chatter in the dugout.

"Maybe when you get back in there," he said to Killebrew, still out with a bad knee, "we'll get going again."

"I hope so," said Killebrew. "But don't underestimate yourself. You've done a tremendous job."

On May 17 the Twins took a record of eleven wins and twenty losses to Cleveland to meet the Indians. Allison, still trying desperately to inspire the team, went hitless in his first two times at bat. After the second failure he returned to the dugout with anger flushing his face.

"I know what I'm doing wrong and I can't help it," he said to Killebrew. "I'm overanxious. I'm lunging at the ball."

"Quit carrying the whole team on your shoulders," Killebrew said softly. "Just go up there and get a hit."

"Easy to say, hard to do," said Allison, but he knew Killebrew spoke the truth.

Jim (Mudcat) Grant was on the mound for the Indians when the fifth inning opened, and he proved a little wild. He walked Bernie Allen and hit Rich Rollins with a pitch. Zoilo Versalles then responded to this opportunity by drilling a home run into the left-field stands to bring home three markers.

But the rally wasn't over. Len Green also walked and Bob Allison was up. When Grant delivered a fat pitch down the middle, Allison clouted it into the left-field seats 370 feet away to bring in two more runs.

"Did I look like I lunged that time?" he asked Killebrew after he had circled the bases.

"You've got your swing back," said Killebrew.

Apparently this was true. In the seventh, Allison was leadoff batter against relief pitcher Jerry Walker. He found a pitch he liked and blasted it 450 feet into the left-center stands!

In the eighth inning Len Green cracked a single to center. The next two Twins were easy outs, and Allison left the batter's circle and approached the plate. This time Ron Nischwitz was the opposing pitcher.

Nischwitz looked the big slugger over and decided he was no guy to toy around with. He tried to catch the outside of the plate with a slider but missed for a ball. He curved the next one for a strike. Allison, swinging his bat in threatening arcs as Nischwitz studied him from the mound, swung at the next one. It was a foul in the stands back of third. The count was now one ball and two strikes. Nischwitz tried one just outside, but Allison let it go by. Two and two.

The fifth pitch was a high hard one, and Allison pulled it to left. It rose dramatically and fell into the seats for his third home run of the game!

The Twins' 11–4 win was almost forgotten in the clubhouse as reporters gathered around Allison. It was the first time that Allison had hit three home runs in one game. It was also the first time in the history of the Twins. And it was only the third time in the history of a Griffith-operated organization (Senators and Twins). Goose Goslin had performed the feat in 1925, and Jim Lemon had managed it in 1958.

Slowly, as the month of May moved along, the Twins began to show renewed signs of life. Killebrew got back in the lineup and responded with some long-distance clouting. Other bats on the team began to boom. And Allison continued to give rival pitchers fits, especially in the clutch.

An example occurred on May 28 when the Washington Senators visited Bloomington. The game was close all the way, and when the last half of the ninth inning came around, the score was tied at 3–3. Ron Kline was serving them up for the Senators and had managed to hold the big bats of the Twins at bay.

Len Green spurred the Twins' hopes by opening the ninth with a double down the left-field line. Vic Power worked Kline for a walk, and suddenly there was a ready-made opportunity to win the game.

It was up to Allison.

Bob glanced down the third base line before he stepped into the batter's box. With two runners on and none out and only one run needed to win, there was a chance he would be asked to bunt the runners along to second and third. But he got the hit signal instead and stepped up to the plate, waggling the bat.

Kline fed him a pitch outside for a ball. The next one was a fast ball, and Bob fouled it back. A curve, breaking away, caught the outside edge of the plate for strike two. The next pitch was a slider, away, and the count was two and two. Kline went to the fast ball then, and Allison went *for* it. He drove the ball high into the stands to win the game, 6–3.

There was great jubilation in the clubhouse after the game. One of the Twins' players said, "We've got a few other good clutch hitters on this club, so I think we better call Allison Mr. Double Clutch!"

Bob just laughed it off.

"Forget that clutch stuff," he said. "I'm just swinging and trying to win ball games like everyone else."

On June 5 Allison kept up the bombardment with his fifteenth homer to help beat the Kansas City Athletics, 4–0. At this time he led the club with fifteen homers and thirty-nine RBI's.

Early in June the Twins began to climb in the standings. Most of their success was due to the fact that the team was once more winning games with the long ball. The statistics were surprising. Home runs were producing 45 percent of the Twins' runs!

By June 12 the Minnesota Twins were again a respected team

in the American League. They had skyrocketed into fourth
place. But even more important, they were only two and a half
games out of first! The Chicago White Sox were leading the
league, followed by the New York Yankees in second and the
Baltimore Orioles in third.

And Calvin Griffith was again saying, with more hope this
time, "We'll be up there at the finish."

13

Calvin Griffith sat behind his highly polished desk in the front offices of the Minnesota Twins and answered questions put to him by a sportswriter. He commented on the team's chances of winning the pennant, on individual players, on prospects among the farm players and various other matters. When the conversation turned to Bob Allison and his ability to hit in the clutch, a smile broke across the president's face.

"You know, Bob had his first year in 1959 in Washington," he said. "Every year since, we've had offers from other clubs who want Allison. They've been big offers too—tough to turn down sometimes. But I resisted them all. I'm convinced Allison is one of the greatest hitters of the game."

"Then you don't anticipate trading him any more?"

"No. He's at his peak and we intend to hang on to him."

As if to verify the accuracy of Griffith's statement, Bob Allison went to work on some Tiger pitching on June 26. The game was played at the Minnesota ball park, and the Twins built a 3–1 lead off Bill Faul by the fourth inning. In the fifth Allison slammed a 390-foot homer into the left-field seats. Later in the game he collected another. They were his eighteenth and nineteenth of the season.

But Allison's contribution to the Twins' fast climb in the standings was not limited to hitting only. One night in late June the Twins were playing in Washington. In a 6–2 win over the Senators, Allison made an unbelievable catch of a drive by Bo Osborne, actually climbing the screen in right field to snag a ball that had home run written all over it. It was a key catch that clinched the Twins' victory.

By June 30 the Twins were in second place, only one and a half games behind the league-leading Yankees.

On July 9 the All-Star Game, played at Cleveland's Municipal Stadium, interrupted regular league play. Bob Allison was chosen on the team this time, but batted only once and failed to hit. The National League won, 5–3.

Allison returned to league conflict inspired by the fact that the Twins were drawing a bead on first place and anxious to help them attain that lofty goal. But it is often when things seem to be going right that something happens—and it did to Allison.

The Twins were in Los Angeles to do battle with the Angels. Allison got up the morning before the first game of the series with a slight chill racking his body.

"I don't feel good," he told Killebrew. "I've got a fever or something."

"Maybe it's a summer cold coming on," Killebrew said. "Why don't you ask Mele to rest you today?"

Allison shook his head stubbornly. "Not if I can trot out on that field," he said.

Allison played that day with a temperature of one hundred. When he was examined after the game, doctors told him he had a virus infection and that he would have to take it easy.

"I'd hate to miss any games," Allison said.

"You're going to miss one tomorrow," said Mele, who was not anxious to imperil the health of his biggest clutch hitter.

Actually, Allison missed the next two games. When he returned to the lineup he felt weak and shaky. For the rest of the month he was in and out of the lineup. He felt continuously weak, and he lost fourteen pounds and much of his strength. As a result, his robust hitting fell off.

It was not until almost a month later that Allison showed a flash of his oldtime effectiveness. The Twins were in Boston to take on the Red Sox. In the fourth inning Allison took aim at the convenient left-field wall and hoisted one over it for a home run off Jack Lamabe.

The two teams were locked in a 4–4 tie when the Twins came to bat in the top of the seventh. Harmon Killebrew opened the frame with a single to center. Don Mincher singled to right, Killebrew stopping at second. That was enough for Lamabe, and reliefer Dick Radatz came in.

It was Allison's turn to bat, and he watched closely as Radatz took his allotted warm-ups. Radatz had always been a particular nemesis for Allison. It was a rare thing indeed when Allison managed a hit off the fireballer. Bob could think of a dozen pitchers he would rather be facing in this critical situation.

Radatz fired a smokeball down the middle for a called first strike. Allison turned to the umpire.

"Did you really see that one?" he asked.

"It was a blur, but it was over the plate," said the ump calmly.

Allison stepped back into the box. Radatz toed the rubber, fired another blazer. This time Allison saw the blur. He swung his bat at it. There was a sharp crack. Seconds later the blur was going in the other direction, bouncing between the left and center fielders for a double. Killebrew ambled home with the go-ahead run. The hit ignited a five-run rally that permitted the Twins to defeat Boston, 9–5.

In the clubhouse a happy Allison said, "I guess my slump is really over when I can get a hit off that guy. It's my first this season."

About this time the Minneapolis–St. Paul newspapers began calling Allison and Killebrew the "home-run twins" of the Minnesota team. A good-natured rivalry had emerged for home-run leadership of the club, with Allison and Killebrew tied at twenty-five each.

Actually, there seemed to be more interest in the home-run race among members of the press than between the two participants. Killbrew had won the home-run title in 1962 with a resounding forty-eight, and there was speculation that Allison might take the title away from the big square-shouldered slugger in 1963.

"I wouldn't want to predict anything," Allison explained patiently to sportswriters. "Harmon might win it again or I might win it. But actually it doesn't matter. The thing that matters is winning ball games. Neither of us is particularly concerned about the home-run title. We're both going up there and swinging—that's all."

Killebrew shared Allison's opinion completely. "Whether you're competing with a player from a rival club or your own," he said, "you just go out and do the best you can each day. As far as I'm concerned, I hope Bob hits a hundred. Chances are we'll win some ball games that way—and that's the important thing."

But Allison's tribulations were not over. On August 6 another misfortune befell him, knocking him not only out of the home-run race with Killebrew but out of the lineup as well. In a game with Los Angeles, the Angels' Dean Chance hit a finger on Bob's left hand with a pitch. The finger was cracked, and Allison was out of the lineup for ten days.

Allison fretted on the bench. His dedication to baseball and the team he played for was so great that it was agony to remain on the bench, useless to the team. Since he was unable to play, he did the next best thing—tried to encourage his teammates and keep them fired up during tough, hard-fought games.

It was August 16 before the finger was healed sufficiently to permit Allison's return to the lineup. He celebrated the occasion by blasting a home run in a Minnesota victory over Baltimore, 13–3.

Then came a memorable August 29 when the Twins rewrote the record book in a fantastic doubleheader with the Senators in Washington. When the long day was over, the Twins had whipped Washington twice, 14–2 and 10–1—but that was only a small part of the story. In administering the two beatings, the Twins had put on the most awesome display of power seen in the American League in many years.

They hit twelve home runs in the two games, eight in the first and four in the second. This bombardement set three new records and tied one. The doubleheader, coupled with previous games, put the following records in the book:

The Twins broke the major league record for most home runs in three consecutive games with fifteen.

They broke the major league record for most home runs in four games with seventeen.

They smashed the American League record for most home runs in five consecutive games with eighteen.

They tied the major league record for one game with eight homers in the opener. The eight home runs were divided among six players—Killebrew and Power had two each, and Allison, Hall, Allen and Rollins had one apiece.

Then, just to prove the game wasn't a freak, the next day Allison and Killebrew hit back-to-back homers in defeating the Chicago White Sox, 5–3. It was Allison's thirtieth round-tripper and Killebrew's thirty-third.

During September, Killebrew drew ahead to win the home-run title again. But this fact bothered Allison not at all. Despite a virus infection and a broken finger, Allison had managed to put together one of his most satisfying seasons. He batted .271, the highest average he had attained in the majors. He hit thirty-five home runs, the most he had hit in either his major or minor league career. And he had ninety-one RBI's to his credit.

Although Bob Allison found a natural satisfaction in his 1963 performance, he was nettled by the fact that the Twins had finished third, one slot behind the previous year's second-place finish. Not only that, but they had ended up thirteen games behind the pennant-winning New York Yankees—and this sizable gap worried Bob.

"We've got a good team," he said to Betty one day. "Maybe we need to strengthen a spot here and there, but so does every team. I really thought we could win the pennant this year, but it didn't work out that way. Maybe we're just one or two players away from a team that can go all the way."

"Next year might be the Twins' year," said Betty, always ready to buoy his hopes.

"It could be," said Bob, "although I don't know where we're going to get those one or two extra players we need."

Bob could have saved himself some worry about the matter, because Calvin Griffith, Sam Mele and the rest of the Twins' brass were working on it. By the time Allison reported to spring training at Tinker Field in Orlando again, the Twins had brought up a new player who was to become a sensation in 1964.

This young man's name was Tony Oliva. And he was to take Bob Allison's position in right field away from him!

14

At a time when a spectacular spring training could have come in handy, Bob Allison failed to have one. But the Twins did all right as a team. Before the Grapefruit League games were over, Minnesota established itself as the hottest team in Florida.

The Twins started out by losing a considerable number of games, but then they went on a winning streak that saw them post a 16–10 overall exhibition game record, the best in the American League.

There were many good reasons for the Twins' fine exhibition season, but one stood out above all others. Tony Oliva, the Cuban rookie, was making his presence felt with some sensational hitting and brilliant outfield play. It gave Sam Mele a problem. He already had three fine outfielders in Allison, Green and Killebrew (who could play in both the outfield and infield). But Oliva was making it impossible for Mele to ignore him. At last the manager made his decision. He approached Allison, a first baseman's glove in his hand.

"Try it on," he suggested.

Allison looked puzzled. "What do you mean, Sam?"

"I want you to play first base this season," Mele said. "I remember you did pretty well back in 1961 when you played the bag awhile. I think you'll do well there—and I've got to get Oliva in the lineup."

Allison took the change without argument. "If you think it will help the team," he said, "I'm all for it."

"Thanks, Bob," said Mele, grateful that the big slugger had taken the change in stride.

Allison went to work at first base and learned all over again the necessary moves around the bag. Griffith, watching him, nodded his head with satisfaction.

"He's okay out there. And he'll improve the more he plays. With his desire, he could play almost anywhere."

But apparently the Minnesota fans took a dim view of the change. Vic Power was a popular player with Minneapolis–St. Paul fans, and letters began to pour into Griffith's office.

Why take Power off first base, they wanted to know. Put Power back in and play Allison in the outfield where he belongs. Oliva's just a rookie. Allison's an experienced outfielder. You're benching a long-ball hitter like Power to gamble on a rookie who might not hit.

So the arguments went. But what the fans did not realize at that point was the fact that Tony Oliva was an exceptional player indeed, and both Griffith and Mele sensed that he would help the club tremendously if he played regularly.

The pleas of the fans were therefore ignored, and when the Twins opened the 1964 season against the Indians in Cleveland, the outfield consisted of Tony Oliva in right, Len Green in center, and Harmon Killebrew in left. The infield had Bob Allison at first, Bernie Allen at second, Zoilo Versalles at shortstop, and Rich Rollins at third.

The Twins won their opener, 7–6, and although Allison failed to get a hit in four times, he handled seven chances flawlessly around the bag.

As the season got into full swing, Allison proved himself to be as adept around first base as he had always been in the outfield. And the switch to first didn't seem to lessen the all-out manner in which he always played baseball either. An example occurred in a game against the Senators in Washington.

It was the sixth inning and Allison was on first as the result of a single. Harmon Killebrew lashed a ball toward John Kennedy, the Washington third baseman, who threw to Chuck Cottier to force Allison at second.

As Bob came down the base line he could see that he would be out by a good distance. But he also noticed that Cottier had cut inside the bag to take the throw—and the thought went through Allison's mind, *I've got to take him out of there to kill the double play.*

Allison went in hard, crashed against Cottier's legs, and upset the second baseman. The slide saved the inning and permitted the Twins to score three times.

"When that big guy came down the base line," Cottier said afterward, "I could hear thunder."

"He shakes the ground up pretty good," was Mele's comment.

On the day before the Twins' opener at home, the Minneapolis Apollo Club gave the team a "Welcome Twins" luncheon at the Leamington Hotel in Minneapolis. The next afternoon the opener was rained out.

In the dugout, watching the rain fall, Allison commented about his shift to first base.

"I imagine the fans aren't very happy about me taking over first base from Vic," he said. "I expect there'll be some booing. The first time I make an error the fans will get on me. And if I make an error that costs a game, the heat will really be on. But I'm not going to worry about it."

Actually, the fans' reaction turned out to be mild. It was true that they liked Vic Power around the bag, but Allison was a big favorite too, and most fans were pleased to have Bob in the lineup rather than out of it entirely.

And, in the first home game, Bob helped his standing with the fans by playing errorless ball in a Minnesota triumph over Washington, 7–6.

In the first two weeks of the new season, however, the Twins failed to impress. The team played only .500 ball, and the power for which the Twins were noted did not materialize.

Then came May 3, and suddenly some of the Twins' dormant power made itself felt. In an extra-inning game against the Athletics in Kansas City, the Twins went into the eleventh inning with the score tied, 3–3. Dan Pfister was the hurler for the A's as Tony Oliva strode to the plate to open the eleventh.

Oliva promptly slammed one of Pfister's pitches into the right-field stands. Bob Allison then came to the plate and tagged Pfister for a second home run. After that both Jimmie Hall and Killebrew hit one.

The four successive home runs not only won the game for the Twins but tied a major league record shared by the Cleveland Indians and Milwaukee Braves.

Despite a slow spring training, Allison was hitting well now that the season had started. A few days after the record-breaking four-homer game, the Twins clashed with Kansas City again at Metropolitan Stadium in Bloomington. Again the Twins' famous power asserted itself.

That day the Athletics jumped on the Twins as if they were going to run them out of the park. They built up an early 7–1 lead and seemed on their way to a lopsided victory. But by the time the seventh inning came around the Twins had cut the lead to 7–6, on home runs by Rich Rollins, Jim Hall, Don Mincher and Bob Allison.

The last of the seventh was a key inning. Reliefer Jack Aker was pitching for the A's, and Versalles worked him for a walk. Rollins struck out, and when Tony Oliva hit a double-play grounder to second baseman Wayne Causey, it looked like curtains for the Twins. But the usually reliable Causey let the ball get through him, and there were runners on second and third with one out.

With first base open, the Athletics decided to walk Hall purposely, loading the sacks and creating a possible play at any base.

Aker concentrated on the next hitter—Bob Allison. He wanted to keep the ball low and force Allison to hit one on the ground for a double play. Stretching, glancing at the runners leading off the bags, Aker pitched. It was a strike, low across the knees. The next pitch was too low, for a ball. Allison then fouled one against the screen.

Ball one, strike two. Allison dug in at the plate. Anything remotely resembling a strike had to be swung at now.

Aker went up with his arms, brought them down, hesitated, delivered. It was a fast ball, just above the knees. Allison swung. He was a little ahead of the pitch, but not too much. The ball was a line-drive double into the left-field corner that scored three runs.

The game ended in a 10–8 victory for the Twins. During the three-hour slugging match the two teams had produced seven home runs, nineteen hits, fourteen strikeouts and thirteen walks. But Allison's ringing double had been the key hit that put the Twins ahead to stay.

Five days later, the Twins put on another awesome display of hitting. This time the Chicago White Sox were the victims on the Twins' home grounds.

The Twins clobbered Chicago pitching for an assortment of hits including six home runs. In the first inning, with Gary Peters on the mound for Chicago, Rich Rollins walked, Allison drew a pass, and Harmon Killebrew rapped his eighth homer of the season into the left-field stands. In the third, Zoilo Versalles led off with a home run. Rollins then walked, Allison lashed a single to center, and Don Mincher blasted another homer. In the fourth, Rollins got into the act by hitting a leadoff home run.

Oliva walked and then Allison clouted his ninth homer of the season into the left-field seats. In the eighth, Killebrew brought down the curtain with his second homer of the day.

The Twins whipped Chicago, 15–7, Allison had three-for-four, and his home run tied him for the league leadership with Jim Hall and Rocky Colavito of Cleveland. The Twins were now in fifth place.

Sam Mele was more than pleased at Bob Allison's performance at bat and in the field.

"Allison has been showing his leadership qualities again," he said. "He has supplied the field generalship the infield has needed. He's been playing first base far better than I had expected, but even more important, he has been giving directions to the pitchers which have helped a great deal. He's also given Oliva a lot of help in right field by moving him in position to play the hitter."

"His hitting hasn't suffered either," a sportswriter remarked.

"Not a bit. And he's improving every day around the bag. Before the end of the season I'm sure Allison will be rated one of the most valuable players on the team."

This appraisal seemed to be general among not only baseball men but the fans and sportswriters as well. Dick Cullum, sports columnist for the *Minneapolis Tribune,* said it perfectly in his column one day. He posed the question:

"Would you care to name the four or five best baseball players in the American League?"

Then he went on to nominate Bob Allison as one of them. He pointed out that Allison could play any outfield position as well as first base.

"Few players can match his desire to win or his concentration on the job," he summed up. "He is a thinking player and a great competitor."

Still, despite the efforts of Allison and many of the other players, the Twins were not thriving. In early June they fell into a hitting slump and by the middle of the month found themselves

still in fifth place, but now seven games behind the league-
leading Chicago White Sox.

Mele was naturally dissatisfied, held clubhouse meetings,
chewed out the team for lax play. Calvin Griffith fidgeted in his
office and finally decided that measures had to be taken to snap
the team out of it.

On June 11 came news that startled everyone on the club.
The Twins had traded both Vic Power and Len Green to the
Los Angeles Angels. In return they had secured the contracts
of infielder Jerry Kindall and infielder-outfielder Frank Kostro.

The shock of the trade seemed to spur the Twins briefly,
for two days later they won two games from the Washington
Senators by scores of 6–5 and 9–2. Allison had one homer in
each game, and this stretched a hitting streak he had going to
fifteen games in which he had hit safely.

Then, on June 16, came another shocker. The Twins sent
pitcher Lee Stange to the Cleveland Indians in return for Jim
(Mudcat) Grant.

"That's what we needed—a good right-handed pitcher," said
Mele. "We think the two trades are going to help this club get
back on the beam."

"It looks like no one is indispensable," remarked one of the
Twins.

But the trades had little immediate effect on the won-lost
column. The Twins continued to slip. Not only did they lose
ball games, but they lost them in unforgivable ways. Their play
was indifferent. They made mental rather than mechanical
errors. Outfielder threw to the wrong base or failed to hit the
cutoff man on throws from the outfield. Pitchers failed to cover
first base on balls hit to the right side, and on occasion Minnesota base runners used poor judgment.

Finally Mele called a clubhouse meeting and blew his top.

"You're playing shabby baseball," he said, "and I'm not going
to tolerate it. Those who don't play heads-up ball from now on
will be fined. I'm going to be sole judge of misplays. And let

me tell you one thing more—fines are going to be more than fifty dollars!"

Despite their lax play, there were three players on the Twins team that other players thought deserved a spot on the American League All-Star team. Bob Allison, who had been selected as a utility outfielder by the manager in 1959 and 1963, was this time chosen by his fellow players as a starter. Selected with him were Harmon Killebrew and Tony Oliva.

But the remarkable thing about the selection of Allison was the fact that he had won the nod from his fellow players *as a first baseman!*

"I guess I've passed the test at first base," Bob said happily. "I never thought I'd make it. This time, being selected by fellow players, gives me a bigger thrill than the other times."

15

Before the All-Star Game was actually played, Allison enjoyed another good day at Metropolitan Stadium. The Twins were behind the Chicago White Sox, 3–2, when Minnesota came up in the bottom of the seventh inning. Allison and Killebrew connected for back-to-back home runs off knuckleballer Hoyt Wilhelm to put the Twins ahead, and they won the game, 5–3.

Allison was now hitting .324, but when a sportswriter asked him to account for his lofty batting average, Bob made no bones about the fact that luck was a factor.

"In order to hit .300," he said, "you must be lucky and have a lot of good hitting streaks like I'm having now. The ball has to fall in for you and you have to get a few breaks. For example, against Pedro Ramos the other night I got a single that luckily went between his legs and over second base. The last time up I got a double when I actually hit a bad pitch. I also hit two balls off the end of the bat against Dick Donovan recently, and both dropped in for hits."

Despite this modest explanation, the fact was that Allison was hitting the ball hard and often. A few days after his explanation to the sportswriter, the Twins met the Boston Red Sox at Fenway Park in Boston. For the first three innings neither team scored. Then, in the top of the fourth, the Twins broke loose with one of those rare scoring innings that leave the opposing team demoralized.

Harmon Killebrew opened the inning with a walk. Allison doubled to right center, and Killebrew scored all the way from first. Jim Hall grounded out, but Earl Battey got an infield hit and Allison moved to third. Jim Snyder then lined a single to right, scoring Allison. Jim Grant flied for the second out, but Zoilo Versalles doubled to left field to score Battey. Rich Rollins singled to right, scoring Snyder and Versalles. Oliva was hit by the pitcher, and Killebrew walked for the second time in the inning.

Allison then hit his second double of the inning to score Killebrew and Oliva. Hall ended the uprising with a ground ball to the infield.

It was a big seven-run inning for the Twins, with Allison's two doubles driving in three. Later Allison homered when the game was out of Boston's reach, making it three-for-four and six runs batted in. The score was Twins 14, Boston 3.

The next day the Twins bombed the Red Sox again, 15–9, and Allison got two-for-four to boost his average to .342.

On July 4, Tom Briere, sportswriter for the *Minneapolis Tribune*, wrote an article that stirred speculation. He said Calvin Griffith considered Allison, with his leadership qualities, to be "managerial timber." This caused some eyebrow raising among the fans, but Griffith immediately explained the statement.

"Don't get me wrong," he said. "I'm not talking about now. I just think that of all the players on the roster, Allison strikes me as best qualified to manage in the future."

Allison was naturally pleased by the comment and the confidence it exhibited. When asked about it, he said, "I haven't given the future much thought, but I'd like to remain in baseball in some capacity."

The All-Star Game interrupted the league schedule at this point, and Allison played seven innings of the big game. Unfortunately, his hot bat was cooled off by Don Drysdale and Jim Bunning, and he went nothing-for-three. The Nationals won the game, 7–4.

On July 9, following the All-Star break, Minnesota traveled to Kansas City for a shot at the A's. For six innings a rookie named José Santiago had the Twins eating out of his hand. The score was Kansas City 1, Twins 0, and it looked as if the Twins' sluggers would never solve the young pitcher's delivery.

Allison came up in the sixth with no one on base. He had failed to hit in two previous attempts, but Santiago was not taking the big broad-shouldered slugger lightly. He pitched with great care, keeping the ball outside to Allison, running the count to two-and-two. With an even count he tried to curve Allison, and Bob swung. The ball traveled like a shot into the left-field stands, tying the score. Don Mincher then came up and hit the rookie for another homer, and that was the ball game— 2–1. It was Allison's twenty-second round-tripper of the year.

About this time of the season both Allison and Tony Oliva, who was doing a remarkable first-year job, were hitting well over .300. Newspapers began to point out that the two hitters were in a race for the batting title.

But Allison didn't agree. "It's too early—much too early— to think about a batting title," he said. "If I'm still close in the last month I might start to think about it. But right now, we're all just trying to win games."

"Yes," said Oliva in his Cuban-slanted English. "Sometimes I get hits, sometimes Allison. The average, she go up and she go down."

About the middle of June the Twins had an off-date, and an exhibition game was scheduled in Winnipeg, Canada. The scheduling of exhibition games in midseason, especially by a club that is in the pennant race, has always been open to question. It's possible to lose a key player with an injury suffered in a game that has no importance, or the entire team might benefit by a day's rest rather than by playing a meaningless game. In the case of the Winnipeg appearance, the game seemed to work a hardship on the Twins.

The Twins were on an airplane for six hours during the night and arrived in Winnipeg at 6:30 A.M. They "hit the sack" at the hotel at 7:00 A.M., but had to get up in time to play the game. Then they had to fly back to Minnesota.

When American League action resumed for them, the Twins promptly lost eight games in a row. They looked like a tired and uninspired team, and when a sportswriter asked Allison what he thought caused the general slump, the big hitter said what most of the players were thinking.

"The Winnipeg exhibition game might have caused it," he said. "We were dead tired."

It was not until July 24 that the Twins won another game. They beat the White Sox on homers by Allison, Versalles and Frank Kostro, all of them hit off Juan Pizarro.

But then the Twins lost two more, skidding to sixth place. Before the slump was over, the record grew to sixteen losses out of eighteen games.

Both Allison and Killebrew, rooming together, were concerned about the Twins' ungraceful slide.

"I wonder what's wrong with us?" Killebrew asked one night as the two sat in their room.

"We're not hitting, for one thing," said Allison.

"I know. But *why* aren't we hitting?"

"That's hard to say. Maybe we're tired." Allison stretched his long legs before him. "You know, Harmon, the breaks have a lot to do with it. Oh, I'm not alibiing. What I mean is, you have to make your own breaks in baseball to win. We aren't doing this. We've beaten ourselves too many times lately. All we can do is play heads-up until the slump ends."

Meantime, Mele started experimenting with the lineup to put some punch in it. Mele wanted to give Don Mincher, a young first baseman with a lot of hitting promise, a bigger try.

"I'm moving you back to right field," he told Allison. "I've got to get some hitting in the lineup, and I want to try Mincher on the bag."

"That's fine with me," Allison said agreeably. "Whatever will help the club is okay."

Nothing much helped, though. The club played listless ball during the month of August and failed to gain ground on the leading teams. The Twins were greatly in need of something to inspire them, and on August 18, when they arrived in Washington for a series with the Senators, they were told that they would visit the White House and meet President Lyndon B. Johnson.

It was a high experience for all the players. They met with the President of the United States in the State Dining Room at the White House. President Johnson shook hands all around, and then he posed with the players for photographs as flashbulbs popped.

In his dry Texas humor, President Johnson quipped, "I'm not really used to this. Since Lady Bird started traveling, I don't have many pictures taken any more."

Following the visit to the White House, Allison hit his twenty-ninth homer of the year at the stadium. But he slumped badly thereafter, not getting his thirtieth until August 30. Between August 18 and 30 he hit a lowly .150—six hits in forty times at bat—which dragged his average down to .286.

This discouraging time was followed by an injury to his hand in the latter part of the season, and Allison collected only two more homers during September. Still, despite all his personal difficulties and the troubles of the team in general, he managed to post a highly creditable year. He finished with a batting average of .287, had thirty-two homers, and batted in eighty-six.

The Twins, after a strong second-place finish in 1962 and a third-place slot in 1963, had tumbled to sixth place—twenty full games behind the New York Yankees, who again stowed away the pennant.

"We should never have finished sixth," Allison said sadly to Betty. "We've got enough good players to finish much higher than that. But we weren't playing up to our potential. Next year it's just got to be different."

Apparently Calvin Griffith and the rest of the club officials thought likewise. They were bitterly disappointed at the strange collapse of a potentially strong team, and Griffith was in a mood to do something about it. And he did.

First, shortly after the season ended, he rehired Sam Mele, thereby making it crystal clear that he felt the blame for the Twins' bad showing did not lie with the manager. At about the same time he signed Billy Martin, formerly a Yankee and Twin player, to a coaching contract.

"We've got to shake things up," he said. "Our club last season suffered the worst collapse of a potentially promising team in American League history. Billy Martin is explosive—which is why we signed him as a coach. We expect him to build a fire under the Twins in 1965."

While all this was transpiring, Bob Allison, Harmon Killebrew, Bill Dailey and Earl Battey took off for Alaska to hold some baseball clinics for young boys. They were given a royal welcome by Alaskan citizens. The four players held clinics in both Fairbanks and Anchorage, and they found young boys in that far-north state as interested in baseball as those in the Twin Cities. And once, during an off-moment, the players were introduced to baseball Alaskan-style—on snowshoes!

"That's a lot worse than playing on solid ground," Allison remarked, almost convulsed by his efforts to hit the ball and run the bases with the ungainly snowshoes on his feet.

"I don't think I'd hit .200 in the Alaskan League," grinned Killebrew.

Although the players had a good time on their visit to Alaska,

much of their evenings was devoted to serious discussions of
their business—baseball.

"I don't know what was wrong with us last season," said Allison, "but I know we have to forget it. We've got to go south
next spring determined that we're going to run every other
team right out of the league. All-out is the only way to play
this game."

Bob Allison was stating his credo. Bob knew it and so did
his fellow players. There was a general nodding of heads. Yes,
next year was going to be different.

16 ⚾

When the players reported to Orlando in the spring of 1965, they found a great improvement in Tinker Field. The infield had always been uneven, with soft spots and pebbles that created hazards for the players. Two years before, Killebrew had suffered a wrenched knee when he slipped on a soft spot, and Earl Battey had been injured a number of times on the treacherous playing field.

This year the Minnesota club had taken action. The entire field had been resurfaced with soil shipped from Minnesota. It required three hundred and fifty cubic yards of dirt to do the job, but the field was in beautiful shape when the players arrived in camp.

"We'll think we're playing at the Met," said one player, referring to Metropolitan Stadium in Bloomington.

Bob Allison arrived with his usual enthusiasm and started practice with the dedication of a rookie. Sportswriters covering the camp, however, looked with some doubt at the team as a whole.

"They look sluggish," said one. "They look like they don't care if the season ever opens."

"They look beaten already," said another.

Billy Martin, the new coach, was quick to dampen this kind of thinking.

"Don't worry about this team," he said. "They'll straighten out when the exhibition games start, and when the season's opener arrives we'll be ready to play!"

After a few days in camp, manager Sam Mele approached Bob Allison.

"I'm going to put you in left field this year," he said. "I'm experimenting with Killebrew at first. Oliva will be in right and I may platoon Andy Kosco and Jim Hall in center."

"Any way you want to work it," Allison agreed.

The exhibition games soon got under way, and despite Martin's prediction, the Twins did not look like a winning ball club. The hitting was almost nonexistent, the pitching fair only in spots, and the fielding left much to be desired. The team looked uninspired and sluggish.

As Calvin Griffith sat in the stands shaking his head, the Twins lost game after game. Griffith and Mele talked about the problem on several occasions.

"It's not so bad that they're losing, it's the way they're losing," said Griffith. "I'd like to see a little more effort."

"They'll be all right when the season starts," Mele said.

"I'd like to see some evidence of it down here," snapped Griffith.

As if the limp and ragged play was not enough, there were nasty rumors circulating and hurting the club. Billy Martin spent half his time denying emphatically the rumor that he was after Mele's job. Mele spent time denying the same rumor.

Don Mincher, reserve first baseman who had been replaced at the bag by Killebrew, made it quite clear that he was displeased.

"If they aren't going to play me, I'd like to be traded," he said bluntly.

There were other beefs too. Jim (Mudcat) Grant told Hal Lebovitz of the *Cleveland Plain Dealer* that the Twins' brass was giving special treatment to its stars, with particular emphasis on Allison and Killebrew.

"I'm not referring to Sam Mele," he said, "and I'm sure the front office doesn't give the stars special treatment consciously. But they do it. They're concerned only with a couple of players, and the rest of us are just around."

With this sort of dissension on the team, the expected happened. The Twins' play on the field deteriorated, and as Griffith quickly noted, they not only lost games but lost them with uninspired and inattentive play.

An example occurred in a spring game against the New York Mets. The Twins were nursing a one-run margin when the Mets managed to get runners on second and third with two out in the fourth inning. Jim Hickman, the next hitter, sent a grounder to the left of Zoilo Versalles for a two-run single. Mele, thinking that Versalles had loafed on the play, yanked him from the game.

"Don't go in the clubhouse either," Mele told Versalles. "Sit on the bench. Maybe you'll learn something."

Versalles' face reddened with anger. "I'll do it for Martin," he said.

"You'll do it for me!" snapped Mele. "And that back talk will cost you one hundred dollars!"

"Why not two hundred?" Versalles shot back.

"Okay. It's two hundred!"

"Why not three hundred?" Versalles persisted.

"All right, I'll make it three hundred!"

Versalles turned on his heel and sat down on the bench. After the game Mele explained. "I don't say Versalles should have gotten that grounder. I don't know if he could have or not. But I know he could have made a stronger attempt. All I ask is that each player give me his best effort. Some of the guys are putting out one hundred percent and some are not. Those that aren't are going to be fined."

It was a sad state of affairs, and the rumors of dissension were at their height as the team quit its Florida base and moved north for the opener with the New York Yankees in Bloomington.

The state of the weather in Bloomington was almost as bad. Minnesota had endured one of its toughest winters, and a week before opening day the temperatures were under thirty degrees and the groundkeepers were shoveling snow off the field and trying to melt the ice around the edges. As the opener neared, fans began to buy tickets, hoping against hope that the Twins could get started. But it looked barely possible.

Just before the season began, Calvin Griffith received a telegram. It was from A. E. Hagberg, president of the Greater Fairbanks Chamber of Commerce in Alaska. The tongue-in-cheek wire explained that temperatures in Alaska were ideal for baseball and that if the Twins wanted to move their opener up to Fairbanks they were welcome to do so.

But the weather did moderate somewhat before opening day. On April 11 the Twins were again honored by the Minneapolis Chamber of Commerce at a welcome banquet at the Radisson Hotel. The next day they faced the Yanks on the field.

The Twins had managed only an 11–15 record in exhibition games, and there was much apprehension among Twins fans as to where the team might finish in 1965. The *Minneapolis Tribune* reported that spirit on the club must be maintained by one or two holler guys, and pointed out that the Twins had none. "Manager Sam Mele is a quiet-spoken type," the article said. "Catcher Earl Battey is on the mellow side. Harmon Killebrew is the same. Rich Rollins makes an attempt to be heard from third base, but he yells in a shrill soprano. Shortstop Zoilo Versalles is better versed in the Spanish tongue. Second baseman

Jerry Kindall has injected most of the holler into the infield, but one voice can only go so far."

The Twins, despite rumors of dissension, lack of spirit and general sluggishness, still managed to get off on the right foot in the opener by edging the Yankees, 5–4, in an eleven-inning game. That started things. Doing a complete about-face, the Twins battled the Chicago White Sox for first place right from the starting bell, with first one team holding an edge, then the other.

The Twins had come alive and were playing heads-up ball!

Bob Allison, almost always a good spring hitter, got off to a raging start. He had two-for-four in the opener and went on to bat .500 for several games. On April 17 he got his first home run of the season off Dick Donovan in a game against Cleveland, helping the Twins to a 3–0 win. By April 21 Allison was still hitting .500, with eight hits in sixteen times up. He slacked off from this torrid pace, but on April 30 he was still hitting .385.

And the Twins were already establishing themselves as a definite pennant threat. They were in second place, only a half game behind the Chicago White Sox.

The two teams were at loggerheads through the first part of May and finally, on May 11, the Twins whipped Chicago, 9–4, and took over sole possession of first place.

On May 14 the Twins battled the Athletics in Kansas City in a game that showed there was still plenty of fight left in the team. Bob Allison's father and mother came over from Raytown to take in the game that night, and as was always the case on those occasions, Bob wanted to do well. But in the first part of the game, things didn't work out his way.

The fourth inning was a good example of how things were going. The Athletics were at bat. The score was 0–0 and the A's had a runner on third with one out. Bert Campanaris was the hitter.

Campanaris lifted a high foul fly toward the left-field corner, and Allison crossed the foul line to get it. With a runner tied up at third, it would have been smarter to let the foul ball drop. But Allison caught it instead, and the runner on third trotted home easily.

As soon as he made the play, Allison knew he had done the wrong thing. In the dugout after the inning was over he said, "I just plain goofed. I don't know what compelled me to catch that fly. I know the next time I'll let it drop."

The one run assumed frightening importance as the game went along, and it began to look as if Allison might be the goat in a Twins loss. After six innings were completed the A's were still leading by a 1–0 score. Their pitcher, John O'Donoghue, was meantime baffling the Minnesota hitters. Allison struck out the first two times up, and the walk back to the dugout each time seemed endless.

In the last of the seventh the Athletics scored two more runs, and the way O'Donoghue was pitching, this looked like more than enough to win.

"We've got two innings to pull this one out," somebody on the bench remarked.

Jim Lemon, the Twins' batting coach, stood with his foot on the top of the dugout steps.

"Quit trying to knock it out of the park, you guys," he said. "Meet the ball where it's pitched."

In the eighth inning Bob Allison strode to the plate with Jim Hall on base. Lemon's words rang in his ears, and he decided that if O'Donoghue pitched him outside again, as he had on two other occasions, he would try to go to right field with the hit.

O'Donoghue pitched, and sure enough, it was outside—too far outside, however, to be a strike. Allison dug his right toe into the dirt and swung his bat in threatening arcs. The pitcher stretched, glanced at Hall dancing off first, delivered. The pitch was on the outside edge of the plate.

Bob reached out and hit it. The ball traveled like a shot into right field, and to Allison's surprise it carried all the way to the stands for an opposite-field home run!

Allison rounded the bases and jogged into the dugout. As he passed Lemon he said, "I hit it where it was pitched."

"Nice goin', Bob," Lemon said, grinning.

Allison's long belt put the Twins in a position where they had a chance to win the game in the ninth—and they did. They scored three more runs to salt the game away, 5–3.

After the game Bob's father shook his hand in the clubhouse.

"You usually don't hit well in this park when the family is watching," he said, "and when you struck out those first two times I thought you would never hit one. But that one in the eighth was a big one!"

"I guess maybe there's a little added pressure when you and mother are watching," Bob admitted. "Anyway, that one in the eighth felt good."

But the Twins, having achieved first place, didn't stay there long. They went into a hitting slump in mid-May and fell three games behind the Chicago White Sox.

Even though it was early in the season, certain pessimists were already writing them off as a pennant contender.

"For a team with all the power they got," said one, "they certainly can go into the doggonedest hitting slumps!"

But what the critics didn't mention was that any team with Minnesota's power can break loose with an awesome display of it in almost any given game. And the Twins did just that on May 25 when they clobbered the Red Sox in Boston, 17–5, hitting five home runs. Allison, Battey, Versalles, Oliva and Kindall were the long-ball clouters in that one.

The next day they hit three more homers—by Allison, Killebrew and Oliva—to whip Boston 9–7, and the victory put them right back in first place again.

As the month of June got under way, Sam Mele began to practice a theory that he held about pennant winners.

"I don't think you can win a pennant these days with a nine-man lineup," he said. "It takes twenty-four or twenty-five players to win a pennant. You have to rest people, substitute others. No one on this team is going to play *every* game."

In June, Don Mincher began to fill in occasionally at first base for Harmon Killebrew. Jerry Zimmerman substituted for Earl Battey, Joe Nossek edged Jim Hall out of the lineup—and Sandy Valdespino, up for the first time with the Twins, took over left field from Bob Allison.

"Maybe Sam's got an idea," Allison conceded. "A rest here and there might help."

June was a tense month in the pennant chase, with the Twins and White Sox trading first place back and forth. Right on their heels, should they start to lag, were Detroit, Cleveland and Baltimore.

But even more discouraging from the Twins' standpoint was the fact that a series of injuries started in June, forcing Mele to make even more lineup changes than he would have liked —and this series of injuries was to mount to almost catastrophic proportions before the season was over.

Some of the changes forced on Mele during that tragic month of June were not for the best, and one day after a particularly sloppy game by the patched-together Twins he moaned, "I don't know who I'll use tomorrow. Maybe I might play one of the sportswriters."

"Or the bat boy?" grinned a reporter.

"Or the bat boy," said Mele, not grinning.

The series of illnesses and injuries piled up frighteningly. They were of such magnitude and frequency that they would have knocked a lesser team right out of the running. But the Twins showed an amazing ability to fight their injuries—substitutes rushed into a game came through in critical situations, players with minor injuries that could have kept them on the bench insisted on playing. The team spirit, which had seemed so lacking during spring training, was now a vital factor in keeping the Twins' pennant hopes alive.

Harmon Killebrew, knowing that Mele would like to get big Don Mincher's bat in the game, offered to switch to third base so that Mincher could play first. When Jerry Kindall was injured, Mele responded by shifting Rich Rollins to second, Killebrew to third, and putting Mincher in at first. Jim (Mudcat) Grant, who heartily disliked starting games and also relieving, nevertheless volunteered to do so. Jim Kaat, a victim of tendonitis in his pitching arm, missed one turn but insisted on pitching despite soreness.

Versalles, accused of lax play in the spring, played with two leg bruises, a sore foot and a pulled groin muscle. Oliva stayed in the lineup despite two swollen knees. Earl Battey, taking a beating behind the plate, was knocked out of the lineup seven times but came right back for more. Jim Hall suffered a knee injury. Jerry Kindall was out two weeks with a bad hip. Pitcher Dave Boswell went to the hospital with mononucleosis. Grant pitched over knee trouble. And Camilo Pascual missed several turns because of a painful pulled back muscle.

During one nightmarish stretch of games, Mele had to use eight different infield lineups in eight days. He also had to start relief pitchers on the mound, and on most occasions they came through with stellar performances.

It seemed that no amount of bad luck was going to stop the Twins in 1965!

During this trying time, Bob Allison began having troubles of his own. He suddenly found himself in one of those unexplainable hitting slumps when nothing would fall safe for him. When he had gone to bat seventeen times without a hit, Mele finally benched him.

"A rest may do you some good," Mele said. "Valdespino will take over awhile."

Allison got back in the game as a pinch hitter on June 23 when the Twins met a charged-up Cleveland team. The Twins were in first place, one game ahead of the White Sox, but Cleveland had won ten games in a row and was making a strong bid to overtake the leaders.

In the early stages of the game Cleveland took a 2–1 lead over the Twins. Floyd Weaver was on the mound for the Indians and looked perfectly capable of holding the Twins in check. But in the fourth inning the Twins began to peck away at Weaver and placed two men on the bases.

"Grab yourself a bat," said Mele to Allison.

Allison walked to the plate as a pinch hitter and looked Weaver over carefully. He didn't wait long. The first pitch was a fast ball and Allison took his cut. The ball dropped into the left-field seats for a three-run homer that put the Twins ahead, 4–2. They eventually won the game, 6–3, and halted the Indians' ten-game winning streak.

Chicago won that day too, which added to the importance of the Twins' victory, for it kept them in first place.

"It's always good to end a hitting slump with a home run," Allison said in the clubhouse, "especially when it's an important game."

Despite the clutch home run, however, Mele did not permit Allison to play every game. He platooned Allison and Valdespino in the early days of July, using Valdespino against right-handed pitchers and Allison against southpaws.

A good ballplayer with an enthusiasm for the game never likes to ride the bench, and sitting out games was a grinding experience for Allison. Finally he asked Mele about it.

"Why aren't you playing me every day?" he inquired.

Mele had an answer. "When you get in there and start swinging like you can, we'll start you every day," he said.

"But, I—"

"Look, Bob." Mele brought out the records. They showed that Allison had had only three hits in thirty-four times at bat from June 15 to July 4. During that time Bob hit only .088, and his overall batting average had dropped from .288 to .256.

"That tells the story," said Mele.

Allison had to admit that it did.

Sam Mele gave Bob Allison a chance to "get in there and start swinging" on July 5 when the Twins tangled with Boston in a doubleheader at Minnesota. Allison made the best of the opportunity. In the first game he collected three hits out of five tries against Boston hurler Earl Wilson, sparking the Twins to a 6–2 win. In the second game he got a hit off Dave Morehead in the fourth, stole second with one of his menacing slides, and came home when catcher Mike Ryan heaved the ball into center field. The run was important, since the final score was 2–0. Allison also collected three walks in the game.

The two wins increased the Twins' first place lead to one and a half games over the hard-charging Cleveland Indians.

Then, just when it appeared that Allison had worked his way into the lineup again, misfortune fell. The next day the Twins played Boston again. It was a big day because Vice-President Hubert Humphrey was in the stands. When Allison came to bat in the first inning against the Red Sox's Jerry Stephenson, he was looking forward to extending his hitting streak and bringing his batting average up to a more satisfactory level.

But Stephenson threw a pitch inside, and as Allison tried to get way from it, he felt an electric pain in his right wrist as the ball hit him. Immediately Dr. William Proffitt, the team physician, trainer George Lentz and Sam Mele were at the plate to see how badly their prize slugger was hurt. The wrist was red where the ball had struck it and was swelling visibly. There was a vibrating pain up Allison's arm that he couldn't ignore.

"Better have it x-rayed," Dr. Proffitt said.

Allison was escorted from the field, and as he walked to the dugout he saw Mele substitute Sandy Valdespino. Bob was half-angry at himself for letting the inside pitch hit him. Just my luck, he thought, when I was beginning to hit again.

Allison was taken to St. Barnabas Hospital in Minneapolis where the injured right wrist was x-rayed. The report turned out to be better than Bob expected, judging from the pain, but was not as good as he would have liked.

"Bob has a bone chip in the wrist," said Dr. Proffitt. "It's a very small chip and I think the wrist will heal quickly. He'll be lost to the club for about five games, but he probably can begin swinging a bat again during the All-Star recess."

While Allison sat forlornly on the bench nursing his injury and his feelings, Valdespino and Joe Nossek platooned in left field. There was only one ray of light in his dark situation. The Twins kept winning, and by the All-Star break on July 13 they had built themselves a three-and-a-half-game cushion over second-place Cleveland. Baltimore was four and a half behind in third, with Chicago six games out and Detroit trailing by seven.

Bob Allison would have enjoyed participating in the All-Star Game in 1965 because it was played for the first time in the Twins' home stadium. Six Minnesota players did appear—Killebrew, Hall, Battey, Grant, Versalles and Oliva. Killebrew contributed a booming homer to the cause of the American League, but the Nationals squeaked through to a 6–5 victory.

Actually, Bob did not get back into action until July 17, and when he did start to play again he found that the injured wrist was still sore and hampered his swing. Allison got one hit in three attempts in his first game after the layoff, but the Twins lost to the Kansas City A's, 5–4.

Still, despite the nagging soreness in the wrist, Allison played some remarkably solid games. On July 18 Bob gave a graphic example of how good fielding and smart base-running can be every bit as important as slugging in the winning of ball games.

The Twins were playing the Angels and the score was tied, 4–4, in the seventh. In the Angels' half of the seventh Allison found himself suddenly chasing a long fly to left field that looked as if it would fall into the seats—or at least bounce off the screen. Allison timed the flight of the ball perfectly, went high in the air and snagged it in the webbing of his glove. The catch kept the score tied at 4-all.

The importance of this dazzling catch was emphasized by what happened when the Twins came to bat in the top of the eighth. Allison opened the inning with a sharp single to center —at least, it should have been a single. But as he took the turn at first, Allison noticed that the Angels' center fielder, José Cardinal, was handling the hit in an unhurried fashion by tossing a looping throw to second base, rather than firing the ball in. Allison kept going and slid into second, stretching the hit into a double.

Sam Mele gave orders to play for the one run, and Jerry Zimmerman laid down a perfect sacrifice bunt, moving Allison to third.

One out and the go-ahead run on third.

Sandy Valdespino was the next Minnesota hitter, and he drew a pass. This brought up Joe Nossek with runners on first and third and one gone.

Nossek watched two quick strikes go by, and on the next pitch Valdespino, a fast man, broke for second. Nossek swung at the pitch, trying to drive it behind the runner, but he struck out. Allison, meanwhile, had broken for the plate.

Bob Rodgers, the Angels' catcher, threw the ball to second

to nail Valdespino, but shortstop Jim Fregosi cut off the throw and fired it back to Rodgers. Allison put on the brakes. He was trapped between third and home!

Allison did some fancy jockeying, back and forth along the third base line, until he forced an error. A throw by Rodgers bounced off Fregosi's glove and dribbled away—and Allison raced home with the go-ahead run.

It proved to be the winning run when the Twins won the game by a narrow 5–4 margin.

"I thought I was a dead duck," Allison admitted after the game. "Usually you can't figure on them throwing the ball away, but sometimes it happens and you have to play out the string. And this time it worked."

"They were probably scared to death Allison would throw a slide at them," grinned one of the players.

Three days later the Twins locked horns with the Boston Red Sox in a doubleheader at Fenway Park. The first game was a seesaw affair that finally ended in an 8–6 victory for the Twins. The second game was similar—only worse. At the end of the eighth inning the two teams were tied, 8–8.

Rich Rollins was the first man to come up in the top of the ninth for the Twins. He singled to center. Again the Twins tried to play for the one run, but this time it didn't work. Tony Oliva laid down the bunt, but it was too hard and the Sox forced Rollins at second. Oliva was safe on the fielder's choice.

Killebrew kept the Twins' hopes alive by rapping a single, and Oliva wheeled his way around to third. Jim Hall then went in to run for Killebrew.

There were now men on first and third and one away, and that was enough to dictate a change in Boston pitchers. In came Dick Radatz, the big reliefer often called the Monster. He owned a fast ball that could be mighty dazzling when he was right. And Allison was the first man to test him.

Bob stood at the plate with his bat on his shoulder as Radatz delivered a blazing strike on the first pitch. Having tasted success with that one, Radatz tried it again. But this time Allison swung and connected. He lined the ball to deep center field, far over Jim Gosger's head, for a triple. Hall and Oliva romped home with two runs to make the score Twins 10, Boston 8. Moments later Allison raced home on an infield error to make it 11–8. That's the way it ended.

The next day the same two teams went at each other in another memorable struggle. They battled on even terms, and when the seventh inning opened the score was 4–4. In the top of the seventh Frank Quilici, playing second base for the injured Jerry Kindall, was safe on an infield error. Jim Grant bunted Quilici to seccnd. Versalles walked. Pitcher Dave Morehead then struck out Rollins.

Men on first and second, two out.

Pitching with great care to the dangerous Killebrew, Morehead finally walked him, loading the bases with two away. Now he was up against it. He couldn't afford to walk Bob Allison, nor could he feed him anything good to hit. Allison waited patiently for his pitch, and when it came—a high fast ball—Bob lashed it into the stands for his fourteenth home run of the season.

In the ninth inning he hit his fifteenth.

"Home runs are always nice, but they aren't everything," Bob said later. "The important thing was that I batted in five runs for the day."

The Twins had won the game, 11–5.

Even though Minnesota had to present a patched-up lineup throughout most of July, they continued to win. By July 30 they were still clinging to first place, with a four-game margin over Baltimore, now in second. All over the league there was open speculation about the Twins' chances.

"I doubt if they can go all the way," said the pessimists. "There are two months to go, and I don't think they've got the pitching to stand up that long."

"They've played over all their injuries so far," said the supporters, "so if they can finish the season healthy they should walk off with it."

Bob Allison opened the month of August batting .264. His fifteen home runs were behind his usual pace, but this was because he had missed games and his long-ball hitting had consequently suffered. Anyway, home runs—or the lack of them —didn't worry him. He was getting other hits, often in the clutch, and every hit counted now as the team tried to overcome injuries and stay alive in the race.

The spirit of the club was immense. It was contagious. The Twins were stubbornly determined to win no matter what happened to them.

"This team has exhibited the greatest display of team spirit I've ever seen," said Mele candidly.

Then came August 2, a dark day in the history of the Twins. On that day both Harmon Killebrew and Camilo Pascual were eliminated from the game!

Killebrew suffered a dislocation of his elbow in a collision at first base, and on the same day Pascual was operated on for torn muscles in his back and pronounced unfit to play for at least a month.

After enduring a rash of injuries all year, this seemed like the finishing blow—to everyone, that is, except the Twins. They simply squared their jaws against the series of mishaps and went out to win more ball games. In the clubhouse they posted a sign. It read:

A HERO A DAY KEEPS THE CONTENDERS AWAY

The sign was prophetic, because this was exactly the way the Twins continued to win. Each day a different player would deliver the game-winning hit or make the sensational catch that saved a ball game. So successful were they that within a week after the dismal August 2 the Twins had actually stretched their American League lead to eight and a half games!

During Killebrew's absence from the game, Allison was called upon at times to share the first base job with Mincher. At other times he played left field. He filled in capably at both positions, but in the first two weeks of August his hitting sagged. Allison and Killebrew had been the team's top sluggers, and with Killebrew injured, Bob felt, as he had once before, that a heavier burden was now on his shoulders. He wanted desperately to take up the slack of Killebrew's absence, and as a result he began to press at bat.

Pressing at the plate is not the mark of a poor player, but of a good one. The player without much desire usually doesn't press because he isn't that concerned when the going gets tough. The good player is concerned, and failure under these circumstances is usually due to the dedicated player trying too hard. This was brought out by Mele in an admiring remark about Allison during the August crisis.

"No one is trying harder than Allison," he said. "He's trying to spark this team."

One day late in August, Allison was due to bat in a critical situation in the ninth inning. As he started for the batting circle Mele called him back.

"Sandy," he said, "hit for Allison."

Sandy Valdespino hopped off the bench to select a bat and Allison sat down again. It was a new experience for Bob to be yanked out of a game for a pinch hitter, and it hurt his pride. He sat with a worried look on his face as Valdespino took his place in the batter's box. After the game ended, he dressed slowly in the clubhouse, his mind in a turmoil. Mele came over and eased the situation.

"Sorry I had to do that, Bob," he said. "But you've been pressing so much, trying to help this club, that you look real bad up there at the plate. I want you to try to relax. No one man is going to win this pennant, and you shouldn't feel that its all on your shoulders."

Bob nodded. He could see the wisdom of Mele's comment.

"I guess, with Harmon out of the lineup, I've been trying to take up the slack," he said.

"That's what you've been doing, all right," agreed Mele. "But it'll be better for the club if you try to relax up there."

In the next few games Allison made a studied effort to relax at the plate. Still, he continued to have difficulties. Methodically, he tried to analyze his troubles. He sensed that he was doing something wrong, but he didn't know what. Finally he went to Mele.

"Sam, I'd like to look at some movies of how I was batting in 1963," he said. "Maybe I can detect what I'm doing wrong."

Mele arranged it, and one morning Allison sat in a darkened room and watched his image on the screen. He made note of the widespread stance, the even swing, the follow-through. After a while he decided that his current trouble was with his balance and his swing. He did not seem to be anchored as firmly in the batter's box, and his swing wasn't level and smooth.

That night the Twins played the Yankees at Metropolitan Stadium, and Al Downing was pitching for the Bombers. In the first inning Allison took his position in the batter's box and paid special attention to the smoothness and levelness of his swing. He struck out on a curve ball, but even so, something told him that he had his problem beaten.

"I think I've got my swing back," he said to Killebrew in the dugout.

Allison could hardly wait to come to bat a second time against the fancy Yankee hurler, and when he did, his balance and his swing must have been perfect because he drove the ball into the left-field seats for a home run—his first homer since August 6.

"Nice clout," said Mele as he bounced back into the dugout after circling the bases.

"I think I have the problem licked," Allison said happily.

The next day Bob was like an eager rookie. He took batting practice with more enthusiasm than he had shown for some time, and when the game started he could hardly wait to get to the plate.

His day's work turned out to be highly satisfactory. He hit a double the first time up, sent a line shot at the third baseman the second time up, slammed another double his third time at bat, and finished off the day with a late-inning home run!

But baseball is one of sport's most unpredictable games. Allison hit his seventeenth homer of the season on August 30, and then his big ravaging bat once more failed him. In the first days of September his hitting fell off again, and with the Twins driving to a pennant Mele decided to rest him again. Valdespino took his spot in left field.

Allison's slump didn't stop the Twins. They continued to amaze the league by playing over both slumps and misfortunes. By September 15 they were ten full games out in front of the Chicago White Sox and the Baltimore Orioles, with Killebrew scheduled to be back in the lineup in a week. The American League pennant was all but locked up at that time, but the Twins left nothing to chance. They continued to play every game as if it represented the clincher.

Bob Allison got back in the lineup in mid-September, followed by Killebrew on September 23. On September 26, Jim Kaat pitched an eight-hitter and the Twins clinched the pennant with a 2–1 victory over the Senators in Washington.

There was great excitement and much noise in the Twins' clubhouse after the pennant-winning game, and when a sportswriter talked to Allison about it, Bob summed up the thoughts of many.

"It's a wonderful feeling to win it," he said. "I'm happy for the club and the whole upper Midwest area. I've been playing eleven years to become a champion in something—and here it is. It's great to be with a winner."

The Twins played out the schedule, then, with their eyes focused on the Los Angeles Dodgers, of the National League, who would be their rivals in the World Series. The Minnesota

fans flocked to the box office for tickets to the first World
Series ever played in Minneapolis–St. Paul—and had Metropolitan Stadium been twice as big, it could have been filled.

Allison finished the season with a record that was a little
below par for him, but which most players in the American
League would have been happy to call their own. He batted
.233, had twenty-three home runs, and batted in seventy-eight.
He had missed twenty-seven games.

But the important point to Allison and all the others was that
the Twins had been able to overcome tremendous disadvantages
all season long to emerge with the pennant. And to add frost-
ing to the cake, Tony Oliva grabbed the batting championship
for the second year in a row, and Zoilo Versalles was in due
time voted the league's Most Valuable Player.

18 ⚾

"I've always wanted to play in a World Series. I just hope I can make a contribution."

Those were the words of Bob Allison as the day drew near for the first game of the 1965 World Series between the Minnesota Twins and the Los Angeles Dodgers. For seven years of his eleven-year career, Allison had been a major leaguer with the Washington Senators and the Minnesota Twins. In those seven years his team had finished eighth, fifth, seventh, second, third, sixth—and now first. Being a member of a pennant winner was a new and exciting experience.

Despite their outstanding show of team spirit in winning the American League pennant, the Twins entered the World Series as underdogs. The Los Angeles Dodgers were 7–5 favorites to take the Series, with the experts predicting that the Dodgers had too much speed and too much pitching for the Twins. With Sandy Koufax and Don Drysdale scheduled for four of the five games, it looked like an insurmountable task for the Twins to overcome.

"We may surprise them," said Mele cautiously.

Bob Allison was not in the lineup for the opening game of

the World Series at Bloomington. With the Dodgers' star right-hander, Don Drysdale, on the mound, Mele decided to go with the left-handed Valdespino—playing the percentages that say a portside hitter has a better chance against a right-hand thrower, and vice versa.

It was a bitter disappointment for Allison to sit on the bench for the first game, but at least he had the satisfaction of seeing the Twins post an impressive victory. Confounding the experts who said Minnesota wouldn't be able to cope with Drysdale, the Twins blasted the stellar right-hander out of the game with a six-run rally in the third inning and went on to beat the Dodgers, 8–2. Jim Grant was the winning pitcher for the Twins.

"Well," said the experts, "tomorrow they get Koufax. That will be a different story."

Mele changed his lineup for the confrontation with Koufax, and Allison found himself back in left field to face the southpaw slants of the famous pitcher. Jim Kaat was selected to oppose Koufax.

For four innings Koufax and Kaat pitched on even terms, and at the end of that time the game was still scoreless. Bob Allison stood in left field awaiting the start of the fifth inning, feeling slightly disappointed with his performance so far. On two trips to the plate he had struck out against the bewildering slants of Sandy Koufax, and so far he had not made the kind of "contribution" he had hoped to make in a World Series game.

Ron Fairly was leadoff man for the Dodgers in the top of the fifth, and he promptly stroked a single into right center. With a man on first and no one out, Kaat pitched carefully to Jim Lefebvre, one of the few power hitters on the Dodger team. But Lefebvre got hold of a fat pitch and drove a vicious liner into the left-field corner.

Allison raced frantically toward the foul line in an attempt to catch the ball. The grass was wet from a pre-game rain, but the spikes of his shoes dug in as he converged on the liner. In his mind's eye, he knew what might happen. If the hard-hit ball got past him and into the corner, it would mean that the Dodgers would have runners on second and third with no one out. This would be a pretty good start on a rally—and the Dodgers were known as a tough club to beat once they got a lead. On the other hand, if he could reach the ball, and hold onto it, he could nip a rally in the bud.

On the mound Kaat watched the flight of the ball with his heart thumping in his throat. He hoped desperately that it would hook foul. There seemed no chance for Allison to get to the ball in time, but Bob was going full tilt in an effort to cut it off. As he raced toward the foul line, Allison noticed that the ball was breaking away from him and dropping fast—and he could see that it would not be foul but would drop just within the playing area.

At the last split-second Allison dived for the ball. He crossed his body with his glove, and as he hit the earth he felt the ball spank into it just inches off the ground. Desperately he squeezed it so that it would not pop out of his glove, and he slid across the foul line on the wet grass as the ball nestled in his glove!

The stands erupted in a great roar at Allison's unbelievable catch. Not only was it one of the greatest catches ever made in World Series competition, but it choked off an incipient Dodger rally and permitted the Twins to go ahead in the sixth and ultimately whip the great Koufax, 5–1.

Allison had a double and struck out three times against Koufax, but his finest contribution was his fantastic diving catch that saved the game for the Twins. In the clubhouse he was besieged by sportswriters and photographers, not to mention his own teammates.

"It was the greatest catch I've ever seen," said Killebrew.

Jim Kaat called it the turning point of the game. "If Allison hadn't gotten to that ball," he said, "they would have had runners on second and third with none out. Who knows what might have happened then? But he did get to it, and it turned the whole game around. We knew it, and I think they did too."

Sam Mele was just as high in his praise. "I might have had to change pitchers with the Dodgers starting a rally if Allison hadn't made the catch," he speculated. "It was one of the finest catches I've ever seen. I didn't think he had a chance for the ball."

Joe Cronin, president of the American League, who had seen many great catches in his time, said, "There's no doubt about it. Allison's catch must take its place among the famous ones of World Series history."

Still tingling with pleasure from two victories over the Dodgers' "unbeatable" aces, the Twins flew to Los Angeles as the Series moved to the West Coast. But here was where things began to fall apart for the Twins. At Chavez Ravine, the Dodgers' Claude Osteen shut out the Twins, 4–0. Allison had nothing-for-three.

That started the skid. The next day the right-handed Drysdale was back on the hill for the Dodgers and Allison was back on the bench. Drysdale got his revenge by beating the Twins, 7–2. Then Koufax came back, determined to avenge his first defeat—and did. He shut out the Twins, 7–0.

A forlorn group of Minnesota players returned home trailing by a game. They would now have to win two in a row to take the Series.

Mele sent Jim Grant to the mound for the sixth game in an effort to hold off the Dodgers. Claude Osteen was back on the mound for the Dodgers.

When the Twins came to bat in the last of the fourth inning the score was 0–0, and Bob Allison found himself at bat with Earl Battey on first base.

Bob's hitting had not been sensational—he had struck out seven times in the Series—but Osteen still respected the big slugger. Working with care, he toyed with a couple of pitches and tried to get a fast ball by Allison. That was a mistake. When Allison swung he felt the repercussion of bat and ball in his hands and arms—and he knew it was gone. It landed 373 feet away in the left-field seats, giving the Twins a 2–0 lead. Although the Twins added three more runs later, it was all they needed to win. The final score was 5–1, and the Series was even at three games each.

But disaster struck in the final game of the Series the next day—in the form of a superb Sandy Koufax performance. The talented left-hander held the Twins to three hits and beat them, 2–0.

It was a bitter defeat for the Twins. They had surmounted an unbelievable number of injuries to win the American League pennant, and they had stretched the World Series to its maximum seven games before bowing to defeat. But, despite their Series loss, they had enjoyed their most successful season since moving to Minnesota in 1961—and they had won themselves a spot in the hearts of the fans.

Bob Allison's record in five games of the World Series included sixteen times at bat with two hits for a .125 average, the two hits being a double and a game-winning home run. And he had made the single most memorable play of the Series—the incredible catch that saved the second game of the Series for the Twins.

It was, in fact, a crowning highlight to Allison's entire season.

Into every great ballplayer's career a certain amount of rain must fall, and the rain descended on Bob Allison in a mighty deluge in 1966. Virtually no player, no matter how talented, has gone through an entire career without suffering a bad year, and 1966 was the first really futile year in Bob's tenure as an American League star.

It all started in spring training at Tinker Field in Orlando. Bob got away to a slow start, and when the exhibition games began he failed to hit with his usual authority. Still, at that time, Sam Mele was hoping that he could start the season with Bob Allison holding down the left-field spot.

During the 1965 season Mele had experienced great success

in platooning when slumps and injuries forced him to take this course. But he seemed to sense that his luck might not hold during the 1966 season.

"I don't like to platoon," he said once. "I would like to start the season with a set outfield—Allison in left, Hall in center, and Oliva in right."

But Bob continued to have such a bad spring that Mele began to entertain doubts about including him in his opening day line-up. Then, late in the exhibition game schedule, Sandy Valdespino delivered a dramatic game-winning single in a victory over Houston, and Mele, dissatisfied with Allison's work, made his decision.

"Valdespino will start in left field on opening day," he said.

It was a nasty blow to Allison not to start the season in his accustomed position. But he felt sure he would get his chance when the club began to see a lot of left-handed pitching and he made the best of his situation. And Valdespino, fighting for a permanent spot on the team, made things tough for him by starring in the opening game.

The Twins beat the Athletics, 2–1, and it was Valdespino who drove in both runs. The next day Valdespino hit a home run in a 5–3 Twin victory—and Allison entered the game as a pinch hitter and struck out.

To compound Bob's misery, there were a lot of rumors circulating among followers of the Twins that there was a big trade looming. And Allison's name was mentioned all too prominently.

One rumor had it that the Twins had offered a four-player package to Boston for Carl Yastrzemski. The four players mentioned were Dick Stigman, Bill Pleis, Jerry Kindall—and Bob Allison!

Another trade rumor had Dick Stigman going to Kansas City for infielder Wayne Causey.

Finally, a trade was made, but it did not involve Allison. Dick Stigman went to Boston for catcher Russ Nixon and infielder Chuck Schilling. It was a trade of second-line players, and the rumors persisted that a big trade of front-line stars might still be coming.

Naturally, having his name mentioned as trade bait concerned Allison, and he was even more concerned when Calvin Griffith seemed to verify it in a talk with a reporter.

"It's true we offered Allison to Boston for Yastrzemski. We'll trade anybody on the club except Oliva, Versalles and five or six pitchers, if we can get our price. But let me make one thing clear—if we put Allison in a deal it will have to be a big one. Bob's big trouble right now is that he's been guessing and looking for that one big pitch. He hasn't lost his stroke. What he has to do is get up there, swing the bat and quit guessing. I'm sure Allison will get his chance soon. Then it will be up to him to do the job."

Although Valdespino started with a loud noise in left field, by mid-April he had dwindled to a whisper. So Allison got his first start of the season on April 23 against the California Angels in Anaheim.

Allison wanted to make the most of his opportunity—and he did. With the Twins leading California, 1–0, in the top of the fourth, Allison led off the inning against pitcher Marcilino Lopez. The California pitcher was in no mood to give Allison anything good to swing at, and he tried to nip the corners of the plate with three successive pitches. All were wide and the count was three-and-nothing.

Lopez managed to catch the corner with his next pitch, and it was three-and-one. He had to come in with the next one, and when he did, Bob swung. The ball soared dramatically into the left-field stands for Allison's first home run of the 1966 season.

Unfortunately the Twins lost to the Angels by a 4–3 score, but Allison had earned an opportunity to stay in left field.

The next day Allison was in the starting lineup again, and this time he hit his second home run in two days off George Brunet and sparked the Twins to a 5–3 victory over the Angels.

Then, just when it looked as if he would be successful in winning the left-field job permanently, things went wrong. Bob went hitless in four tries in the next game. There were four straight rain-outs, and when the team got back in action in a doubleheader against Washington, Allison went hitless in seven times at the plate.

The next day Valdespino was back in left field.

This time Allison didn't get back into the lineup until May 12. In this game he had two-for-four against the Yankees and made a startling catch of a foul fly. Still, when Mele looked at his overall batting average, he shuddered a little. Allison had four hits in thirty-two times for an anemic .125.

When he went hitless the following day, Mele benched him again. Valdespino wasn't knocking down any walls either, and Mele began to alternate him and Jim Hall in left field. When that didn't work too well, he gave Andy Kosco a chance.

The infield was likewise unsettled. Don Mincher, playing first, found himself in a slump. Finally Mele moved Rich Rollins to third base and shifted Harmon Killebrew to first. When Rollins caught the flu, Killebrew went to third and Mincher came back in.

Once, when Mele couldn't coax hits out of any of the left fielders—Allison, Kosco, Hall or Valdespino—he grew desperate and put Rollins in the outfield. That lasted just one day, during which Rollins had such a trying day as an outfielder that Mele decided never again to subject him to such treatment.

Late in May the harassed manager, who couldn't seem to get any combination working like the Twins of 1965, shifted Tony Oliva from right field to center. He put Killebrew in left and Rollins back at third.

That looked pretty good to Mele, until the improbable happened. Tony Oliva, batting champion for two straight seasons, went into a slump!

So it went for Sam Mele and his Twins in early 1966. And

so it continued. Allison found himself in and out of the lineup as Mele tried to put together a winning combination. But the Twins sagged in the race. They were not hitting, their fielding was so-so, and their pitching was subpar.

They no longer looked like the American League champions.

Sam Mele was reluctant to give up on a player of Allison's stature. Even while Allison was in his April and May slump, he still received more walks than any other player on the team, indicating that rival pitchers had not lost their respect for the big slugger. Besides, when you looked at Allison's record, you could hardly give up on him too quickly. In seven seasons as a major leaguer, he had averaged twenty-eight home runs a year and had batted in an average of eighty-eight runs a year.

As Casey Stengel put it, "You play against that feller and you don't think he's hurtin' you any. Then you look at the figures and he's got eighty or ninety RBI's. I'll take him."

But as June progressed, Allison found himself starting few games. With Mele of a mind to platoon his outfielders, no manager ever had a better chance. Competition for an outfield job was probably as severe on the Minnesota Twins as on any team in the major leagues. The Twins had nine outfielders!

Besides Bob Allison, there were Jim Hall, Andy Kosco, Joe Nossek, Tony Oliva, Cesar Tovar, Sandy Valdespino, Ted Uhlaender and Harmon Killebrew. And with Tony Oliva a fixture in the outfield, this left eight outfielders vying for two jobs in the Twin's garden!

So Mele platooned to his heart's content, the team dawdled in the second division, and Allison sat on the bench, always accompanied by five other outfielders.

Still, it seemed that whenever Allison was called on to play, he came through in good style. On July 4, for example, the Twins were playing the Indians in Cleveland. In the Twins' outfield on this occasion were Killebrew, Oliva and Uhlaender.

At the end of seven innings of play the game was tied, 3–3,

and the Twins were battling to end a seven-game losing streak. The Twins got a runner on base in the top of the eighth with Russ Nixon coming up.

"Allison, go in and hit for Nixon," said Mele.

Allison selected his favorite bat and went to the plate. He waited not at all. He hammered John O'Donoghue's first pitch deep into the left-field stands to put the Twins in the lead, 5–3. Allison's homer turned out to be the key hit in the game as the Twins won, 5–4.

Two days later Allison hit another homer against Cleveland that helped the Twins win, 4–3.

Apparently the inability of the Twins to go with a set lineup hurt them for much of 1966. They continued in the second division for more than half of the year, and they were particularly weak against the Yanks, Orioles and Angels. By mid-July they took account of their record and found they were 40–22 against the rest of the league but only 3–25 against those three teams.

"If they had only split with those three teams," wrote a reporter, "the Twins would be in first place."

There were a lot of "ifs" in the Minnesota Twins' 1966 season. *If* Mele had been able to go with a set lineup the team might have gone all the way. *If* there had been less dissension among coaches Billy Martin, Hal Naragon and Johnny Sain, the team might have prospered. And *if* Allison had played and contributed his usual quota of home runs and RBI's, the team might have finished on top.

But it was not until after the All-Star break that the Twins began to move. In August and September they climbed steadily —from fifth to fourth to third to second. Eventually, with the Baltimore Orioles pulling away from the rest of the league, the race narrowed down to a fight between the Twins and the Detroit Tigers for second place.

It was during the tense days when second place was at stake that Bob Allison reached an important milestone in his career.

It was September 18, 1966, and Allison was not in the starting lineup as the Twins clashed with the New York Yankees in an important game at Yankee Stadium. The Yanks, fated for last place in the American League standings, were nevertheless strong enough to put a crimp in Minnesota's ambitions to finish second. They started Hal Reniff on the mound against the Twins, and for a long time it looked as if Minnesota would never solve the twenty-eight-year-old right-hander's delivery.

The Yanks jumped on Minnesota rookie Jimmy Ollom in the first inning for two runs. Then, with Reniff dazzling the Twins' batters, the score remained 2–0 in favor of the Yanks for six innings. But the Twins pushed over two runs in the top of the seventh and tied up the ball game, 2–2. The score remained deadlocked through the ninth.

In the top of the tenth the Twins started a rally. Harmon Killebrew rapped a double down the left-field line, and Earl Battey walked. Jim Hall, a left-handed hitter, was the next batter coming up. But Steve Hamilton, a left-handed pitcher, was now on the mound for the Yanks, and Mele decided to play the percentages by sending up a right-handed pinch hitter for Hall.

The pinch hitter was Bob Allison. It was a ready-made spot for a clutch hitter of Allison's ability. He stepped into the batter's box, dug his right toe into the dirt, and waved his bat threateningly.

Hamilton fidgeted on the mound, adjusting his trousers, his cap. He gazed in and got the sign, went up with his arms, glanced quickly at Killebrew and Battey on the bases, and delivered the first pitch to Allison.

That was all. Allison swung and the ball traveled like a shot into the right-field stands to put the Twins ahead, 5–2. The Yanks scored one in the bottom of the tenth, but Allison's blast had supplied the cushion necessary to win.

It was a milestone home run for Allison—the 200th homer of his major league career!

The rest of the season was an anticlimax. The Twins finished in second place, one game ahead of the Tigers and nine games behind Baltimore.

It takes only a glance at the records to see that Bob Allison ranks, without question, as one of the American League's top right-handed long-ball hitters. With 200 home runs to his credit, he is the second greatest slugger ever to play for a Griffith-owned ball club (Senators and Twins). Only Harmon Killebrew leads him. He has far outdistanced such sluggers as Roy Sievers, Jim Lemon, Mickey Vernon and Goose Goslin.

But Bob's value as a clutch hitter is even more important than the round-trippers he has produced. He averaged eighty-eight runs batted in per season during his first seven seasons when he missed only a few scattered games, but even this statistic doesn't tell the entire story. It's *when* those runs were batted in that counts, and a great many of them came late in games when the Twins were either tied with their opponents or trailing. This was when Bob Allison was the most dangerous.

Behind the bare statistics, however, lies an even more important story. Bob Allison is more than a good hitter and fine fielder. He is a symbol. Every rookie who puts on a baseball uniform and dreams of becoming a major leaguer can take a look at Allison's career and take heart. His story shows what it takes to get there.

From the time he first played baseball on the sandlots around Kansas City, Bob was a good ballplayer. But when he was finally signed by the Washington Senators and sent out for minor league seasoning, he became just one of many young men trying to climb baseball's difficult ladder. Judged strictly by the statistics, his minor league career was far from impressive. Only in 1958, when he batted .307 and drove in ninety-three runs for Chattanooga, was there any promise at all. Before that, his highest batting average was .256, and the most RBI's he had ever accumulated was fifty-five.

But Bob had one thing many players lack—the one vital

element that was to help him make the grade. That was determination. He was convinced he could do anything he set out to do in life if he simply tried hard enough—and he proved it by overcoming the statistics with an enthusiasm and dedication to the game that couldn't be overlooked by his baseball superiors.

Never satisfied with anything less than perfection, Bob Allison turned himself into a complete ballplayer by sheer effort. He has proved that, given a modicum of talent, determination is the essential ingredient that will turn an average ballplayer into a great one.

And when the inevitable day comes that he hangs up his spikes, that may be the really important legacy Bob Allison leaves to baseball.

WILLIAM ROBERT ALLISON/Born: July 11, 1934

Bats right, throws right
Outfielder-infielder

Weight: 220 pounds
Height: 6 feet 4 inches

Year	Club	G	AB	R	H	2B	3B	HR	RBI	BA	PO	A	E	FA
1955	Hagerstown	122	446	55	114	15	2	5	49	.256	289	24	12	.963
1956	Charlotte	122	344	47	80	10	6	12	55	.233	240	20	11	.959
1957	Chattanooga	125	395	56	97	14	11	2	38	.246	239	8	7	.972
1958	Chattanooga	150	525	84	161	28	9	9	93	.307	372	13	18	.955
1958	Washington	11	35	1	7	1	0	0	0	.200	24	0	0	1.000
1959	Washington	150	570	83	149	18	9	30	85	.261	333	8	9	.974
1960	Washington	144	501	79	126	30	3	15	69	.251	311	13	11	.967
1961	Minnesota	159	556	83	136	21	3	29	105	.245	417	18	10	.978
1962	Minnesota	149	519	102	138	24	8	29	102	.266	287	10	7	.977
1963	Minnesota	148	527	99	143	25	4	35	91	.271	326	11	10	.971
1964	Minnesota	149	492	90	141	27	4	32	86	.287	829	58	12	.987
1965	Minnesota	135	438	71	102	14	5	23	78	.233	247	12	7	.974
1966	Minnesota	70	169	34	37	6	1	8	19	.219	85	3	3	.967
Major League Totals		1115	3807	642	979	166	37	201	635	.248	2859	133	69	.977

Index